当代国际商务文化阅读丛书

Readings for Modern International Business Culture

【英汉对照】

企业帝国
继承权之争
——『商务文化』篇

Corporate Empires' Grappling with
Succession
Business Culture

吴斐　编著

武汉大学出版社

WUHAN UNIVERSITY PRESS

图书在版编目（CIP）数据

企业帝国继承权之争："商务文化"篇：英汉对照/吴斐编著．—武汉：武汉大学出版社，2016.5
当代国际商务文化阅读丛书
书名原文：Corporate Empires´ Grappling with Succession：Business Culture
ISBN 978-7-307-13999-2

Ⅰ.企… Ⅱ.吴… Ⅲ.商务—文化—英、汉 Ⅳ.F72

中国版本图书馆 CIP 数据核字（2014）第 191501 号

封面图片为上海富昱特授权使用（ ⓒ IMAGEMORE Co.，Ltd.）

责任编辑：郭园园　金　军　　责任校对：鄢春梅　　版式设计：韩闻锦

出版发行：**武汉大学出版社** （430072　武昌　珞珈山）
（电子邮件：cbs22@ whu. edu. cn 网址：www. wdp. com. cn）
印刷：武汉中远印务有限公司
开本：880×1230　1/32　印张：10.25　字数：223 千字
版次：2016 年 5 月第 1 版　　2016 年 5 月第 1 次印刷
ISBN 978-7-307-13999-2　　定价：28.00 元

前　言

　　人类社会进入 21 世纪后，国家间的商务往来更加频繁，商务交际手段随着互联网的诞生和电子信息的进步日新月异，国际化企业的文化和理念千差万别，商务话题的表达和沟通能力无疑是人们所遇到的最大障碍。　在我们熟知的生活英语、学术英语之外，商务英语不仅是我国目前从事或即将从事涉外商务人员英语实际应用能力不可多得的辅助工具，更是商务工作人员在这个国际化的高科技时代商务竞争能力、外贸业务素质和英语水平的重要体现。《当代国际商务文化阅读》（英汉对照）丛书以从事国际商务活动所必需的语言技能为经，以各种商务活动的具体情景作纬，将商务精神和商务元素巧妙融合，展示时尚而又经典的商务文化世界流行风，为广大读者提供一套语言规范、内容新颖、涉及面广、趣味性强、具有实用价值、富于时代精神的读物，既注意解决人们在国际商务环境中因遇到不熟悉的专业词汇而无法与外国合作者就工作问题进行交流沟通的难题，又着力解决人们学外语单纯地学语言而缺乏商务专业知识的弊端。

　　《当代国际商务文化阅读》（英汉对照）丛书由 10 个单行本组成：《拥抱新欢亚马逊（Embracing Amazon Service）——电子商务篇

1

（E-Commerce）》、《华尔街梦魇（Nightmare on Wall Street）——商界风云篇（The Business Circles）》、《路易斯·波森的朋克摇滚（The Punk Rock of Louis Posen）——商界精英篇（Business Elites）》、《希波克拉底誓言（Hippocratic Oath）——商务交际篇（Business Communication）》、《强烈的第一印象（A Powerful First Impression）——商务礼仪篇（Business Etiquette）》、《企业帝国继承权之争（Corporate Empires' Grappling with Succession）——商务文化篇（Business Culture）》、《紫色血液（The Purple Blood）——商务心理篇（Business Psychology）》、《多米诺骨牌效应（The Domino Effects）——商务知识篇（Business Knowledge）》、《公开的赌注（Public Stakes）——商务演讲篇（Business Speeches）》、《伊斯特林悖论（The Easterlin Paradox）——感悟财富篇（Comprehension of Wealth）》。　这套丛书的编写旨助帮助读者在国际商务环境下，能够读懂英文的商务信息和商务新闻，并能对某一商务话题的知识有全面透彻的了解，领悟当代时尚商务文化成长的环境和思维方式，提高在全球化高科技时代的商务竞争能力、外贸业务素质和英语交际水平。　丛书中的阅读材料力求做到题材广泛、内容精辟、语言规范，遵循趣味性、知识性和时效性原则，培养读者在商务环境下的英语竞争能力和综合应用能力。　丛书融时代性与经典性为一体，内容经得起时间考验，文字经得起反复咀嚼，保证其可读性。　读者在阅读过程中接收大量的语言输入，为合理组织和娴熟运用英语语言表达自己的思想打下牢固的基础。　丛书的单行本包括以一个主题为中心的 30 篇文章，每篇文章包括题记、英语原文、汉语译文、生词脚注和知识链接。"题记"用丰富生动的语言点评文章的精髓，对文章的内容起到提炼和画龙点睛的作用。"英语原文"主要摘自当代国际主流报纸杂志，具有语言规范、内容新颖、涉及面广、趣味性和时代感等特点。"汉语译文"力求准确流畅，既关注译文的文化语境及其内涵，也重视译文的外延和现当代标志性语言符号。"生词脚注"的难度把握在大学英语六级和研究生英语词汇程度，以帮助读者及时扫清阅读障碍。"知识链接"根据文章内容，或精解一个专业术语，或阐释一种新的商务理念，或介绍叱咤商界的企业或公司，以帮助读者培养游弋商海、运筹帷幄的能力，具备洞悉中西文化的国际视野。

《企业帝国继承权之争》（Corporate Empires' Grappling with Succession）——商务文化篇（Business Culture）给读者展现了一个璀璨斑斓的商务文化世界。　商务文化是生产领域和流通领域中商品经济活动产生的特有文化现象，它随着商品交换的产生而产生，并与商业实践相始终。　虽然它迄今已有悠久的历史，但作为一种社会文化现象，其价值观和行为准则在当代瞬息万变的经济大潮中也发生了翻天覆地的变化。　IBM公司的企业文化是在老托马斯·沃森和小托马斯·沃森父子两代人共同生产经营中创造的，它渗透进IBM人的血液和骨髓。　在全球化环境中衍生的高度结构化和复杂化文化使IBM公司的企业文化仍然在剔除糟粕、吸取精华的传承中与时俱进。　路透社20年来一直在为稳定核心业务和创造一个成长的平台做着不懈的努力，然而，彭博社对传统新闻市场的冲击，从根本上颠覆了"给苦难者慰藉，让惬意者难受"的新闻原则，将路透社逼上了重新打造品牌、转变思维观念的征途。　迪士尼无疑是全球文化产业运作的成功典范，在其文化背后有着一个不断发展、扩充、升级的轮次商业运作模式，使迪士尼抵御市场风险的能力相对于其他媒体集团来说棋高一筹。　相比之下，新闻集团的默多克虽然一直运用他杰出的、战略性的思想精心打造和整合团队机构，但依旧不敌具有强劲品牌和空前多样生财方式的迪士尼。

　　产品和企业的品牌符号在全球文化中承载着品质卓越和责任担当的光环。　万宝路"西部牛仔"代表的是自由精神，大红鹰"V"代表永远胜利，NIKE 的"对勾"代表叛逆的心理，可口可乐的红色代表活力。　令人扼腕叹息的是，全球品牌化的光彩在人们对跨国公司的围追堵截中黯然失色，品牌符号被视为既能造福、又可作恶的强大机构。　可口可乐、麦当劳和耐克之类的品牌已经成为反全球化浪潮的出气筒：愤怒的示威者砸碎了瑞士达沃斯麦当劳出口的玻璃门，踩踏着西雅图的可乐罐。　消费者对全球品牌的认知迫使企业在文化背景下思考全球文化的符号，了解好莱坞和宝莱坞电影、美国有线新闻网和卡塔尔半岛电视台新闻报道、嘻哈音乐和苏非派音乐等世界不同文化之间的区别。

　　文化差异常以一种微妙的方式影响人们的商务行为。　如果美国推销员向沙特阿拉伯的潜在客户推销价值数百万美元的猪皮粘合剂，无疑会被穆斯林文化定位为邪恶的行为。　而德国的工人与监事会的监事几乎拥有同等的代表权，则会让北美体验过基于集体管理的股票持有人的管理人员惊诧不已。　当意大利的轮胎制造商"倍耐力"企图收购其德国的竞争对手"欧洲橡胶"时，文化差异的潜藏挑战使"倍耐力"损失惨重。　肯德基、麦当劳和必胜客在中国早已是家喻户晓的洋快餐品牌，其舒适的环境、周到的服务、良好的卫生条件以及统一的包装深受中国消费者的青睐。　但品种相对单一、

4

与中国人的传统饮食习惯不一致等问题，也造成了这些快餐企业发展的"瓶颈"。美国百胜全球餐饮集团在上海肯德基连锁店率先推出了传统的北京鸡肉卷，肯德基在菜单中增加了四川榨菜和肉丝汤，麦当劳不甘落后，推出了蔬菜海鲜汤和玉米汤。这种卓越的跨文化管理模式既是市场经济发展的产物，也体现了人类与现代生活快节奏的和解。

　　商务文化效应好似"以石投水"，石子激起涟漪，向整个池面漾去，文化就弥漫在整个水面之中，并且渗透在社会生活的方方面面。本书选辑的主要阅读文章包括：改变公司文化之战（The Battle to Change Corporate Culture），全球文化中的品牌符号（Brand Symbols in the Global Culture），企业帝国继承权之争（Corporate' Grappling Grapple with Succession），跨界谈判中隐藏的挑战（The Hidden Challenge of Cross‑Border Negotiations），薪酬的价值（The Worth of Your Paycheck），洋快餐的混合文化模式（A Model of Blended Culture of Foreign Fast Foods），修复世界金融体系（Fixing the World Financial System）等。

　　商务文化，从远古的物物交易中演绎而来，沿着社会进程的坎坷颠簸前行，将沿途的风景塑造得美轮美奂，又为未来布置了永无止境的憧憬和魅力。阅读超凡脱俗的商务文化，让我们跟随时代潮流，追赶文化经济信息、商业模式、企业品牌形象、推广产品市场的商业脚步，享受世界流行文化创造的快乐、荣誉、价值和成就感！

作　者

2016 年 1 月

目　录

目　录

题　记

　　印度经济的崛起过程，是无数古老或新兴家族兴衰起落的大型演义。尽管历经浮沉起落，家族企业在印度经济舞台上扮演的始终是主角。今日的印度，内部竞争骤然加剧，外部世界的全球化狂潮也卷入印度国门，经济自由化使曾经权倾一时的家族企业家们瞬间手足无措。印度名副其实的"商业帝国"信实工业集团就因为继承权的公开纠纷和官司战争让家族企业的前途成为公众瞩目的焦点问题。集团继承人的矛盾在父亲逝世几年后如火山般喷发出来。穆克什认为自己是长子，理所应当继承父亲的全部事业；而兄长实力的不断膨胀，使阿尼尔的资产份额和管理决策的能力逐渐被掩盖，心底的怨恨逐渐加深，甚至将其告上法庭。尽管这个闹剧在母亲的调解下收场，但它也为无数企业帝国继承权之争敲响了警钟。

Corporate Empires' Grappling with Succession

For over a century, family-run business empires have held sway in India, but acrimonious① succession battles are now turning off foreign investors and prompting Indian corporations to adopt post-dynastic strategies. With names such as Tata, Birla, Godrej and Reliance, they are some of the biggest players in the world in industries that range from steel to concrete, autos, telecoms and petrochemicals. Yet some of India's largest conglomerates② are still family affairs, much to the chagrin of investors who have seen some family-run companies implode as the founders have died and their children have squabbled over business empire inheritance. "Badly-run family firms run the risk of not being able to grow profitably and of scaring off potential investors," said Anjan Ghosh, a general manager at ICRA, a unit of Moody's Investors Service that has studied family firms in India.

---

① acrimonious [ˌækriˈməuniəs] *adj.* 恶毒的
② conglomerate [kənˈɡlɔmərit] *n.* 多元化集团公司

2

企业帝国继承权之争

百余年来，家族企业帝国已经统治了印度，但当今激烈的继承权之战使得外国投资者望而却步，迫使印度企业实行后王朝战略。塔塔、贝拉、高德瑞治和信实工业等知名企业都是世界工业的一些最大玩家，它们囊括了钢铁、水泥、汽车、电信和石化等行业。 然而，印度的一些顶级综合性企业仍然是家族企业，当创始人去世时，他们的子女就会在商业帝国的继承权问题上争吵不休，那些目睹家族企业帝国分崩离析的投资者对此十分懊恼。 穆迪投资者服务公司印度投资信息及信用评级中介机构的总经理安健·戈什先生认为，"经营不善的家族企业存在无法增加利润和吓跑潜在投资者的危险"。 穆迪投资者服务公司已经研究过印度的家族企业。

由于面临信用危机的冲击，印度对全球经济衰退的恐惧与日俱增，而家族企业则可能需要快速解决如何处置继承权的问题，否则难以承受全球经济动荡带来的严重打击。 特别是在当前资金难求的市场环境下，企业必须采取专业化运营方针，并制定周密的接班计划，不然将会举步维艰。

As India faces the fallout of the credit crisis and fears of a global recession rise, family-run companies may need to quickly determine how they will handle succession or risk being badly buffeted by a turbulent global economy. Especially in the current market environment where access to capital is such an issue, unless you are professionally run and have a succession plan in place, it will be tough.

Inheritance wars between feuding siblings such as Mukesh and Anil Ambani, the world's fifth and sixth riches people according to Forbes magazine, have tarnished India's allure as a top investment destination, raising risks for investors in a country where corporate legislation and regulation are in their infancy and shareholders largely stand passively on the sidelines. With families controlling 18 of the 30 firms on the benchmark BSE index, the risks are serious.

Certainly, some family-run companies have made ambitious acquisitions recently and taken on global rivals, while others are drawing up tentative succession plans, hiring professionals in leadership positions, divesting assets, and even surrendering control. Private equity firms invested more than $ 14 billion in Indian firms, while foreign funds bought shares in Indian companies worth a record $ 17.4 billion. These welcome signs of maturity are lost in the clamour around the squabbling Ambani siblings and other corporate succession battles. Mukesh, the elder brother, took control of energy and petrochemical giant Reliance Industries Ltd, India's biggest private sector company after the Ambani empire was split, three years after its founder Dhirubhai's

穆克什和阿尼尔·安巴尼是一对有着宿怨的兄弟，他们的继承权之争，削弱了印度作为投资圣地的魅力。 根据福布斯财富榜的排名，他们分别位于第五和第六的位置。 在一个公司立法和监管尚处于初级阶段的国家，这场纷争无疑增加了投资者的风险，股东很大程度上也被动地持观望态度。 印度股票交易所的基准股指 BSE 指数显示，由于 30 家企业中有 18 家由家族控制，风险相当严重。

当然，当其他家族企业还在草拟初步的继承计划、雇佣专业人员担任领导职务、剥离资产、甚至交出控制权的时候，也有一些家族企业最近已经完成了雄心勃勃的收购，甚至接管了全球竞争对手。 印度私人股本公司的投资超过 140 亿美元，而外国资金购买印度公司股票价值创下 174 亿美元的纪录。 这些颇受欢迎的成熟迹象在安巴尼兄弟和其他公司继承战的喧嚣中悄然而逝。 创始人德鲁拜·安巴尼去世 3 年后，安巴尼帝国一分为二，兄长穆克什控制了能源和石化巨头信实工业有限公司，这是印度最大的私人联合企业。 阿尼尔接管信实信息通讯公司、信实投资公司、公共建设及娱乐资产等其他实业。 然而，这对兄弟的持久战一直曝光在媒体的聚光灯下。 最近，孟买市法院的一位法官又听闻以这对兄弟为首的公司为天然气供应而争吵不休，法官已经建议他们去找他们的母亲解决这个问题，不要在法庭上对抗。

牛津分析智囊团在一份近期报告中指出，这种长期争斗也延伸到其他的商业领域，正在对印度的经济发展、其作为顶级投资圣地

death. Anil gained control of mobile services firm Reliance Communications, Reliance Capital and other power, infrastructure and entertainment assets. The two brothers, however, have continued to fight in the full glare of the media. Recently, a judge at Mumbai's city court that is hearing a gas supply dispute between companies headed by the brothers is reported to have suggested they go back to their mother to settle the matter, rather than fight in court.

The feud①, which also extends to other businesses, is causing real damage to India's economic development and its appeal as a top investment destination, and even spilling into the political arena, think-tank Oxford Analytica said in a recent report. "The rivalry reflects fundamental questions of business ethics and threatens to exert a serious impact on the economy, notably in the short term by introducing uncertainty into energy regulation and delaying investment in the gas sector." These and other public spats② and legal battles over succession have put the spotlight on the future of family-run businesses in India, among the world's fastest growing economies.

Most Indian family-run companies date back more than a century to the British colonial era, with the notable exception of Dhirubhai Ambani, the son of a school teacher, who founded the Reliance group in the 1970s. While it is quite common for groups to split to resolve

---

① feud [fju:d] n. 争执
② spat [spæt] n. 争吵

的吸引力乃至政坛造成实际损害。"这种竞争反映了商业道德等基本问题，对经济产生了严重的威胁，尤其是给短期能源监管带来了不确定性，造成了天然气部门的投资延缓。" 印度是世界增长最快的经济体之一，关于继承权的公共纠纷和官司战争已经让家族企业的前途成为公众瞩目的焦点问题。

印度的大多数家族企业可以追溯到一个多世纪前的英国殖民时代，但德鲁拜·安巴尼是个例外。 他是一名乡村教师的儿子，在20世纪70年代创建信实工业集团。 尽管解决企业传承问题时集团分裂是十分正常现象，但在许多案例中，坚持传统或者单纯搁置会阻碍企业的交接计划。 印度商学院的拉玛钱德朗教授认为，"出于本性，人们总是认为事情会进展顺利，不会有任何冲突"。 巴贾吉家族控制了印度第二大机动车生产商的巴贾吉汽车公司及其他公司，其业务也在兄弟之间的矛盾激化下分解。 即便是广受尊重的印度第二大多元化集团、全球第六大钢铁制造商塔塔集团，也还没有确定2012年75岁的主席塔塔退位后的继承人。

互联网内容评级协会在一份报告中称，印度是一个新兴的市场，但公司和管理的立法和制度框架仍然有待发展，在很大程度上缺乏积极的股东文化，所以公司缺少继任计划尤其堪忧。"领导过渡是至关重要的管理和信誉风险"。 按照传统，长子继承家族企业的衣钵，但塔塔先生单身一人，膝下无子。 他说他的继承人可以来自家族之外。 与此同时，创建印度顶级移动运营商巴帝电信的第一代

7

succession issues, in many cases it is simply adherence to tradition or sheer procrastination[①] that hinders planning, said K. Ramachandran, a professor at the Indian School of Business. "It's human nature to assume things will go smoothly forever and that there will never be any conflicts, " he said. The Bajaj family that controls Bajaj Auto Ltd, India's No. 2 motorcycle maker, besides other firms, also split their businesses to end a simmering feud between the brothers. Even the widely respected Tata Group, the second-largest Indian conglomerate which controls the world's sixth-largest steel maker, has not identified a successor to Chairman Ratan Tata, who is scheduled to retire when he turns 75 in 2012.

But the lack of succession planning is especially worrying in an emerging market like India, where legal and institutional frameworks for companies and governance are still being developed and an activist shareholder culture is largely absent, ICRA said in a report. "Leadership transition is a key governance and credit risk." While traditionally, the eldest son inherited the business mantle, Tata, who is single with no children, has said his successor could come from outside the family. Meanwhile Sunil Mittal, a first-generation entrepreneur who set up the country's top mobile operator Bharti Airtel, has appointed professionals at the top of the group alongside his two brothers.

Tougher market conditions may encourage more family businesses to look at succession and exit options seriously, said Thomas, a managing

---

① procrastination [prəuˌkræstiˈneiʃən] *n.* 耽搁

企业家苏尼尔·米塔尔，在公司高层任命了除他的两个兄弟之外的专业人员。

罗斯柴尔德常务咨询公司的主管托马斯认为，市场环境越艰难，越能激励更多的家族企业认真对待继承和退出的选择。"业主们可能会想：我们已经相当成功了，我们真想永远这样做下去吗？或许可以去打打高尔夫。"

企业的独立董事和新一代领导人，他们拥有海外工商管理硕士学位，携带的情感包袱较少，而他们制定的规章制度正在改变企业的理念。托斯卡纳投资私人股本公司的首席执行官夏尔马说："那些孩子尚小的创始人企业家意识到，他们需要资金和管理资源，以维持企业长远发展。也有一些老企业，孩子们不想参与公司的事务，因此他们不得不将企业售出。但是，他们可能不会选择卖给竞争对手，因为这会表明败给他们。他们相反会选择更受人尊敬的私人股本。"近期的交易包括：戈卡达出口公司的第一代创始人将公司出售给黑石集团，兰伯西实验有限公司的第三代业主将多数控制权卖给日本第一三共制药公司。

知识链接 🔍

Reliance Industries 信实工业集团。由德鲁拜·安巴尼创建的信实工业集团是印度最大的私营公司，不仅掌控了国家电力、石油勘探、金融、生物科

director of advisory firm Rothschild. "The owners may think: we've been reasonably successful, but do we really want to do this forever? We can instead play golf."

Regulations such as those requiring independent directors and a new generation of leaders, armed with MBA degrees from abroad and carrying less emotional baggage, are transforming business. "In the case of some first-time entrepreneurs with very young children, they realise they need the capital and management resources to sustain the business long term," said Vishal Sharma, chief executive at private equity firm Tuscan Ventures. "There are also older businesses where kids don't want to be involved, so they have to sell out. But they may prefer not to sell to a rival, as that indicates a failure to them, and instead opt for private equity, which has gained more respectability." Recent deals include the sale of Gokaldas Exports by its first-generation founders to Blackstone and the sale of majority control in Ranbaxy Laboratories Ltd by its third generation of owners to Japan's Daiichi Sankyo Co.

(1,020 words)

技以及电信领域的发展方向，而且在很大程度上左右着整个印度经济。

ICRA 互联网内容评级协会（Internet Content Rating Association）。互联网内容评级协会是家庭网上安全协会组织的成员之一，提供有关互联网安全的一般资讯和意见，其网站是 www. fosi. org。

题 记

　　酒香也怕巷子深。在商家林立、竞争激烈的市场环境中，低调承诺被定义为一张走向被遗忘角落的单程票，只有高调承诺才能适应现代消费者和商机异乎寻常的流动速度。"美国女孩"创造的八个有"思想"的洋娃娃根据不同历史时期的背景，讲述着积极向上、励志感人的故事，高调兑现了公司的承诺；谷歌缩短了搜索时间，帮助客户在网上找到任何他们想要的东西，高调兑现了公司的承诺；悍马公司以独特新颖的设计和舒适简洁的内置空间，为客户提供了一种无可比拟的驾驶体验。只有高调承诺的公司才能够始终如一地实现高调兑现：它们的产品与承诺一样表现可靠；它们架构了获取产品的整套体系；它们能够清楚地理解员工和客户各自的身份。毫无疑问，高调承诺在帮助企业加入具有非凡魅力的品牌行列的过程中功不可没。

Over-Promise Your
Way to the Top

How can you make your products irresistible? Make outrageous claims—and then deliver on them. Rick Barrera is president of Overpromise Inc., a consulting firm that designs and executes differentiating marketing strategies for companies of all sizes. This branding expert tells you why you should and how.

The old cliché in business is that you should under-promise and over-deliver. But in a crowded marketplace, under-promising is a one-way ticket to oblivion①. Because consumers and businesses are moving and shopping at warp speed these days, they won't slow down long enough to fully understand your under-promise. To grab their attention, you must over-promise.

By over-promising, I don't mean you should promise things you can't deliver. Instead, I mean you must make an outrageous claim on which you can deliver. Most companies already have such capabilities, which is why their current customers do business with them. But their marketing teams haven't taken the time to understand exactly why their

---

① oblivion [ə'blivian] *n.* 遗忘

高调承诺助你走向成功

　　如何让你的产品具有不可抗拒的诱惑力呢？ 做出超出常规的承诺，然后再兑现承诺。 里克·巴雷拉是"高调承诺公司"的总裁，这是一家为各种规模的公司设计并执行市场营销战略的咨询公司。这位品牌专家将告诉你为什么和怎样做。

　　做生意有句老套话，那就是你应该少承诺，多做事。 但是在竞争激烈的市场环境中，低调承诺只是一张走向被遗忘角落的单程票。 因为现在的消费者和商机正在以异乎寻常的速度流动和购物，他们不会长时间地放慢脚步，充分理解你的低调承诺。 为了吸引他们的注意力，你唯一的出路就是高调承诺。

　　我所指的高调承诺，并不是让你承诺你不能兑现的事情。 相反，我是让你对于你能兑现的事情做出不一样的承诺。 大多数公司已经具有了这样的能力，这就是他们目前拥有客户和他们做生意的原因。 但是他们的营销团队还没有花时间全面思考，为什么他们目前的客户会真的具备如此的忠诚度，然后清楚地讲述，在这种不一样的高调承诺中，他们具有什么样的独特能力。

　　我在为最近的新书《高调承诺和高调兑现：不可动摇的客户忠诚度的秘密》做调查研究时，惊讶地发现竟有如此多的产品、服务

current customers really stay loyal, and then articulate their unique capabilities in an outrageous over-promise.

While doing research for my most recent book, Overpromise and Overdeliver: The Secrets of Unshakable Customer Loyalty, I was astounded① by how many products, services and companies didn't have an articulated over-promise. If you don't tell customers why they should buy from you, but your competitors do... then guess who gets the customers?

Here are three excellent examples of over-promises you can use for inspiration:

· American Girl over-promises by offering girls dolls that will utterly enchant them... and then over-delivers by giving each doll a fascinating biography.

· Google over-promises by offering everything a customer would want to find on the Web...and then over-delivers with an average search time of 0.2 seconds.

· Hummer over-promises a driving experience that's "like nothing else"...and then over-delivers with an attention-grabbing design, extra comfort and a built-in Hummer community.

So how can you create your own over-promise?

First, start by examining your vision for your company. Why did you start it in the first place? What was missing in the marketplace that you vowed to fix on behalf of your customers? I often find that the essence of a brand can be drawn from a business founder's original thoughts. You could feel it even if you couldn't articulate it. Now's the time to make that

---

① astound [əs'taund] vt. 使惊异

和公司没有清楚地表达高调承诺。 假如你没有告诉你的客户为什么要购买你的商品，而你的竞争对手却这样做了……可想而知，谁争取到了客户？

这里有三个高调承诺的经典案例或许可以帮你激发灵感：

"美国女孩"高调承诺给女孩们提供洋娃娃玩偶，这个承诺使她们神魂颠倒……后来公司又给每个玩具娃娃写了一个引人入胜的传记，高调兑现了它的承诺。

谷歌高调承诺帮助客户在网上找到任何他们想要的东西……后来他们高调兑现了承诺，平均搜索时间只需要 0.2 秒。

悍马公司高调承诺一种"无可比拟"的驾驶体验……公司后来高调兑现了承诺，其出品的悍马系列不仅拥有引人注目的设计，而且还有新颖的舒适感和内置的悍马空间。

那么，你如何创建自己的高调承诺呢？

第一，从检查公司的愿景开始。 为什么从此处开始是当务之急？ 你发誓要代表客户修复市场上缺少的什么？ 我发现，品牌的实质往往来自公司创始人的原始想法。 即使你不可能清楚地表达出来，也能感受到这一点。 那么现在是阐述创意的时候了。

第二，你的产品或服务唯一的、最重要的特征是什么？ 是什么使它独一无二？ 消费者听见公司的名字时，联想或感受到的一个词是什么？ 沃尔沃代表安全。 雷克萨斯代表奢侈。 你的产品会让人想起什么呢？

第三，问一问你的客户，他们为什么买你的产品。 然后再问，他们为什么不买你竞争对手的产品。 根据这两个答案之间的差别，你可以得到一种提示，它告诉你应该高调承诺什么。

articulation.

Second, what is your product or service's single, most important attribute? What makes it unique? What one word do customers think about or feel when they hear your company's name? Volvo means safety. Lexus means luxury. What does your product mean?

Third, ask your customers why they buy your products. Then ask them why they don't buy your competitors' products. In the chasm① between these two answers, you'll find a beacon② that points to what your over-promise should be.

Fourth, ask non-customers why they don't buy your products or services. Then ask why they buy your competitors' products. This pair of questions will give you insight into the misperceptions they have about your product or company, or will point you toward serious shortcomings in your offerings.

Fifth, what emotions do your customers feel when they use your products? Why do customers pay a premium for a Hummer, a Lexus or an American Girl Doll? It's because of the way it makes them feel or because of the way it makes others feel about them. These are powerful brand-building insights you must consider when you're crafting your over-promise.

Once you've done your research and have brainstormed some potential over-promises for your brand, be sure to test them with your customers and your potential customers for effectiveness in both their ability to grab attention and to accurately reflect the actual brand

---

① chasm [ˈkæzəm] *n.* 差别,分歧
② beacon [ˈbiːkən] *n.* 信号灯

第四，问问那些还不是客户的人，他们为什么不买你的产品或服务。然后再问，他们为什么买你竞争对手的产品。这一组问题将帮助你深入剖析客户对你的产品和公司的误解，或者帮你指出产品中存在的严重缺陷。

第五，你的客户在使用你的产品时是什么感觉？为什么顾客愿意为悍马、雷克萨斯或美国女孩玩偶公司支付溢价？这是因为它们带给客户一种感受，或者是让客户体验到别人对他们的感觉。当你在精心策划你的高调承诺时，这些都是你必须考虑的品牌营造的强大内涵。

一旦你做完调查，为你的品牌集思广益，并想出了一些潜在的高调承诺的点子，一定要通过你的客户和潜在的客户检验它们的效果，考察你的高调承诺是否能引起消费者的注意，是否准确地反映了实际的品牌体验。太多的公司会犯致命的错误，他们做出了尽善尽美的高调承诺，但根本没有办法履行这些高调承诺。这会使客户在很短的时间内就发现你不可能兑现你的承诺。当你做出合适的高调承诺时自己也会清楚，因为这种高调承诺会引起客户和员工的共鸣。

现在再来谈一谈高调兑现。我的研究显示了一个清晰的模式，即高调承诺的公司也能够始终如一地实现高调兑现。他们在创造独特的客户体验方面专注三个关键点：产品、系统和人的要素。首先，产品必须与承诺一样表现可靠，关键是合适的设计。其次，易如反掌地获取产品，形成资金、组装、使用、储存、安装和维修等整套体系。如果消费者获得产品时饱受打扰，使用起来又太过复杂，即使是世界上最伟大的产品，其价值也会大打折扣。最后，员

experience. Too many companies make the fatal mistake of creating aspirational over-promises that they can't fulfill. It will take your customers a very short time to find out you can't deliver on your over-promise. You'll know when you've got the right over-promise because it will resonate with both customers and employees.

Now, over-deliver! My research showed a clear pattern in the companies that were able to consistently over-deliver on their over-promises. They focused on creating unique customer experiences at three critical touch points: the product, the systems and the human element. First, the product must reliably perform as promised — appropriate design is crucial. Second, the product must be easy to acquire, finance, assemble, use, store, fix and dispose of — this is the system. The greatest product in the world is worth far less if getting it is a hassle or if it's too complicated for customers to use. Finally, your people — the human element — must clearly understand the role they play in delivering the overall customer experience. How should they dress? What should they say? How should they act? Don't leave these details to chance, or your people will make up their own version of your brand.

Over-promise and over-deliver is a formula that's been proven to be successful by American Express, Pottery Barn, Samsung, Washington Mutual and many other top businesses. If you're willing to invest in the research required to get your over-promise right and the attention to detail required getting your over-delivery right, your brand, too, can join the ranks of the irresistible!

(869 words)

工必须清楚地理解他们在提供整体用户体验的过程中扮演的角色，这就是人的要素。他们应该穿什么？他们应该说什么？他们应该做什么？不要放过这些细节，否则员工会对你的品牌做出自己的解读。

高调承诺和高调兑现是一种模式，美国运通、陶瓷谷仓、三星、华盛顿互惠银行和许多其他的顶级企业已经证明了这种模式的成功。如果你愿意投资，进行达到正确高调承诺所需的研究，关注达到正确高调兑现所需的细节，你的品牌也可以加入具有非凡魅力的品牌行列。

知识链接 🔍

American Girl　"美国女孩"。"美国女孩"是与"芭比娃娃"不同的另外一款占据着不少市场份额的洋娃娃。1986 年，帕莱森特·罗兰德在 45 岁时创办了帕莱森特公司，经营"美国女孩"洋娃娃。"美国女孩"洋娃娃一共包括八个小女孩，每一个女孩都有六本相关的书籍来讲述她的故事，主要根据不同历史时期的背景，描写一个 9 岁的女孩如何获得成长的故事。现在，罗兰德还发行了《美国女孩》杂志及一系列关于友谊和社交的书，创建了位于芝加哥的"美国女孩"大厦，经营着洛杉矶、纽约等数 10 家"美国女孩"专卖店。"美国女孩"品牌的地位已经在无数 7-12 岁的女孩心中根深蒂固。

Pottery Barn　陶瓷谷仓。陶瓷谷仓是一家于 1949 年成立于曼哈顿的设计公司，主营顶级和高端板式家具及软体家具，提供全线家居产品个性化定制。他们追求的设计理念是"家具应舒适、有格调并且品质卓越。或是老式的触感和原创字母的装饰元素；或是颜色既不浮夸也不中立"。

题　记

为了工作而来回穿梭于陌生城市间的一群高端商务人士被人们形象地称为"空中飞人"。频繁外出、飞来飞去是多数商务人士的一种特殊而无奈的生活方式。然而，电子商务和互联网的发展悄然间让他们的生活方式发生了改变：越来越多的商务人士开始选择使用陆地交通工具。传统的商务旅行被赋予了新的内涵，自驾车商务出行逐渐成为时尚。更多的商务人士开着私家车，载着产品四处兜售，不仅享受了工作的快捷和方便，而且通过碳减排实现环境资源的可持续利用和交通的可持续发展。经常开车出行的商务人士带着现代商务必备的上网本、商务手机等科技含量高又功能强大的电子工具，随时与客户、家人联络，了解行业的最新动态，关注国内外大事，为现代社会的生活呈现出一幅多姿多彩的商务旅行画面。

What Goes Around
Comes Around

Business Travel: It's easy to focus on the world of airlines, but most business travel is done on the ground.

There's a musical about business travel opening on Broadway tomorrow night, and there isn't an airplane or an airport lounge in sight. When the curtain comes up on "The Music Man," a revival of the 1957 hit, the stage is filled by a jostling① railroad car crammed with traveling salesmen who sing a patter-song of trade gossip as they haul into Iowa with their suitcases crammed into the overhead bins on a summer's day in 1912.

Writing about the culture of modern business travel, it's easy to focus on the endless issues of the airline world and forget the fact that most business travel is still done the old-fashioned way, on the ground, on wheels — by car, if not by railroad. According to the National Business Travel Association, 51 percent of business travelers used their own car on their most recent business trip, and another 8 percent used a

① jostle ['dʒɔsl] n. 拥挤

24

有失必有得

对于商务旅行来说，人们易于关注航空领域，其实大多数商务旅行依赖于地面交通。

百老汇明晚将上演一场关于商务旅行的音乐剧，舞台上看不到飞机和候机大厅。幕布升起之时，1957年轰动一时的"音乐人"会再次在舞台上绽放光彩，这是1912年夏日的一天，一辆满载旅行推销员的有轨电车横冲直撞，驶往爱荷华州，推销员们把行李箱塞进头顶的行李架，喋喋不休地唠叨着业内的八卦传闻。

人们编写现代商务旅行文化时，易于无休止地关注航空公司的问题，但他们忽略了这样一个事实，即大多商务旅行仍然沿用老办法，依赖地面上的轮子，不是坐火车就是坐汽车。根据国家商务旅游协会的调查，51%的商务旅客在近期的商务旅行中开私家车，另有8%的人用公司的车。

叶萨维奇、佩珀丁&布朗以及扬克洛维奇伙伴公司联合完成的国家商务旅行监测调查显示，超过半数的商务旅行者承认，他们开私家车或公司的车出差，而不是飞往目的地再租用汽车。根据这项调查，所有的商务旅行者中，2%的人坐火车。根据政府的统计数据，30%的铁路乘客是商务旅客，而不是每日往返上班者。

company car.

More than half of business travelers said they used a personal or company automobile on business trips (as opposed to those who flew to a destination and rented a car) , according to the National Business Travel Monitor survey by Yesawich, Pepperdine & Brown and Yankelovich Partners Inc. Two percent of all business travelers traveled by railroad, according to the survey. But 30 percent of railroad passengers, other than commuters, are business travelers, according to government statistics.

"I have to laugh when I run into the ones who go by plane; all they talk about is the number of frequent-flier miles they have, " said Tom Malloy, a self-employed restaurant equipment salesman. He was encountered yesterday afternoon in his late-model Toyota, cell phone in one hand and bacon-cheeseburger in the other, enjoying what he joked was the "businessman's lunch special" in the parking area of a rest stop on the New Jersey Turnpike, about an hour out of New York City. He was bound next for a stop in Maryland on a long trip down the coast that was scheduled to end with calls on businesses in southern Florida.

"You know the number I focus on?" he asked. "Thirty-two and a half cents. That's what the I.R.S. lets me deduct as a mileage expense for business travel this year. Sounds like a little number when you compare it to those guys who say they have, what, nine billion frequent-flier miles — but I put on about 85,000 miles a year. You do the math."

Mr. Malloy made another point about business trips on the ground: "Look, I got my Palm Pilot. With the new technology, I'll be hooked up to the Internet soon, right in my car. I got my cell phone, which works

有失必有得

自助餐设备推销员汤姆·马洛伊说："我碰到那些坐飞机旅行的人就感到好笑，他们只会谈论自己常坐飞机累积的英里数。"我昨天下午碰到他时，他正坐在新款的丰田汽车里，一只手拿着手机，另一只手拿着培根奶酪汉堡，笑称他正在享用"商人的特殊午餐"。此处是新泽西州收费公路一个休息站的停车场，离纽约市大约1小时的车程。他打算沿着海岸长途驱车，下一个停车点应该会是马里兰州，预计在佛罗里达州的南部处理完公务后结束旅行。

他问我："你知道我关注什么数字吗？32.5美分。这是美国国内税务局让我扣除的费用，即今年商务旅行的里程开支。与那些达到90亿频飞乘客英里数的人相比，这个数目听起来真是小巫见大巫。但我一年开了8.5万英里，你算算。"

马洛伊先生对地面商务旅行提出了另一个观点："瞧，我有掌上电脑。这项新技术使我可以在开车时一直挂在网上。我还有随处可用的手机，随时随地可以联系上我。反正我讨厌坐飞机，除非我要去百慕大，几个小时都不能与外界交流。打个比喻说，憋死在水里了"。

和马洛伊先生一样开车旅行的商务人士常常聚集在州际公路休息站和餐馆这样的地方，他们在那里建立了临时办公室，在快餐厅餐桌或汽车的前排座椅上兴奋地打字或热闹地聊天。与此同时，他们的同胞正在3万英尺的高空飞行。马洛伊先生认为，如果真要与外界联系，用"那些时髦的飞机座位手机"也不太方便。这时，马洛伊先生的手机响了，我们不得不停止闲聊。

显然，车轮上的交通局限于区域旅行，或是像马洛伊先生这样的旅行者，远程商务旅行的途中需要多次短暂停歇。一直以来，销

anywhere. I'm never out of touch. Put me in a plane, which I hate anyway, unless I'm going to Bermuda, and I'm incommunicado for hours at a time. I'm dead in the water, so to speak."

Like Mr. Malloy, business people who travel by car often congregate① in places like Interstate rest stops and restaurants, where they set up impromptu offices, typing or chatting away furiously at fast-food restaurant tables or in the front seats of their cars. Their compatriots②, meanwhile, are flying overhead at 30,000 feet and relegated to staying in touch, if at all, "with those cheesy airplane seat phones," said Mr. Malloy, who had to stop chatting when his cell phone rang.

Obviously, transportation on wheels is limited to regional trips, or to those travelers, like Mr. Malloy, whose long-range business journeys require many short stops. Sales people traditionally have formed the bulk of these business travelers. But technology is also spawning a new kind of business travel on wheels. Increasingly, high-technology start-up companies and businesses that operate in the technology sphere are adding fleets of cars and light trucks for business use by their employees. Some younger employees, in fact, have grown so weary of airport delays that they are driving on short-haul business trips — say, between Boston and Philadelphia — that used to be made strictly by air.

Over all, business auto leasing shows a steady growth of 3 to 5 percent a year, said Todd Schreiber, the vice president for marketing at

---

① congregate ['kɔŋgrigeit] *vi.* 聚集
② compatriot [kəm'pætriət] *n.* 同胞

售人员是此类商务旅行者的主流。 但是，科技又衍生出一种新型的车轮上的商务旅行。 越来越多新成立的高科技公司和在科技领域运营的企业，为他们的雇员提供了商用车队和轻型卡车。 事实上，有些较年轻的雇员越来越厌倦航班延误，如果是波士顿和费城之间的短途商务旅行，他们更愿意自己驾车，而以前则一律坐飞机。

联合车队服务公司的营销副总裁托德·施瑞伯认为，总的来说，商务汽车租赁业务每年固定增长 3 到 5 个百分点。 联合车队服务公司是位于达拉斯的第一资本协会的一个部门，负责租赁和管理公司的车队。 他认为，这是一个脱颖而出、急剧增长的领域。 而且，该领域中新科技和老传统的轮子之间正在形成一种奇特的关系。 施瑞伯先生说："新开的小型公司铺天盖地。 我们现在有一个专门的销售队伍，目标直指新兴和中型市场，提供 25～250 辆的车队服务。"

这些新开的公司以小型中间商的组织形式起步，从当地经销商那里租赁 3 辆到 5 辆车便开始营业。 随着业务的增长，他们的业务范围已经超出了地区或国家，销售队伍也不断扩大。 而其他公司则脱离了新兴市场领域，迅速成为实质性的组织。 他们可能以 30 辆到 40 辆车起家，突然之间就拥有 150 辆到 300 辆车。

施瑞伯先生补充说："由于互联网和电子商务在商业中如此巨大的作用，我们还注意到快递服务、小型和中型面包车和卡车租赁的巨大增长空间。 过去，典型的销售人员开着车，拿着产品四处转悠，招待客户午餐，你现在将看到一幅完全不同的商务旅行画面。"

或正如歌剧"音乐人"中老谋深算和厚脸皮的商务旅行者哈罗德·希尔教授说的那样："有失必有得。"

Associates Fleet Services, a unit of Dallas-based Associates First Capital, which leases and manages company-car fleets. But one area stands out for sharp growth, he said. Again, it involves that odd relationship that is growing between new technology and the old-fashioned wheel. "Small start-up operations have just exploded, " Mr. Schreiber said. "We now have a separate sales force that's dedicated to emerging and middle markets — fleets of vehicles from 25 to 250 cars."

These companies started out as small entrepreneurial organizations with maybe three or five cars that they got from their local dealer. As their business has expanded, they've gone regional or national, with an expanded sales force. Other companies come out of that emerging-markets segment and become substantial organizations quickly. They'll start out with maybe 30 or 40 cars, and all of a sudden they have 150 or 300 vehicles.

"With the Internet and e-commerce playing such a big part in business, " he added, "we also see a tremendous area of growth in delivery services, small and midsize vans and trucks. You're looking at a completely different type of business travel now than it used to be with your typical sales person who had a sedan to go out and take products around and entertain some clients at lunch."

Or, as Prof. Harold Hill, the wily and brassy business traveler of the "The Music Man " might have said, "What goes around comes around."

(957 words)

知识链接 🔍

The Music Man 《音乐人》。又名《乐器推销员》，是世界上最著名、最畅销的音乐剧之一。该剧还是百老汇历史上一部从作词、作曲、编剧均由一人包办，上演历时最长的一部音乐剧。这个人就是具有传奇色彩的梅里迪斯·威尔逊。融入了梅里迪斯·威尔逊多年结晶的《音乐人》于 1957 年 12 月 19 日在大剧院首演，顿时犹如一股强气流闯入美国音乐剧界的最前沿。在托尼奖的角逐中，它击败了《西区故事》，成为 1958 年的托尼奖的获奖大户。该剧上演了 173 周，共 1 376 场，巡演时间持续了三年半。最新一版的《音乐人》于 1999 年由当今百老汇著名的编舞家苏珊·斯多曼复排，2000 年 4 月 27 日首演于内尔·西蒙剧院。

题　记

　　迪士尼无疑是全球文化产业运作的成功典范，在其文化背后有着一个不断发展、扩充、升级的轮次商业运作模式，即通过迪士尼的动画制作、主题公园以及品牌产品和连锁经营的三轮收入模式，使迪士尼抵御市场风险的能力相对于其他媒体集团来说棋高一筹。作为传媒巨头的它站在办公室里任凭外面世界风声雷动依然按兵不动，这样虽不能驱使股票价格的变动，但也从一定程度上避免了股票波动对公司实体的间接影响。相比之下，新闻集团的默多克虽然一直运用他杰出的、战略性的思想精心打造和整合团队机构，但依旧不敌具有强劲品牌和空前多样生财方式的迪士尼。默多克的大手笔是斥资并购华尔街日报的母公司道琼斯和并购社交网站MySpace。尽管这些并购被外界认为是非常大胆的举动，但未带来投资者所希望看到的收益。投资者已经开始质疑默多克一厢情愿的报纸行业……

Disney Emerges a Winner

As Murdoch's Dow deal hobbles News Corp., Disney's sales pitch to media stock investors remains the most plausible — for now.

It hasn't been fashionable to be a big, groaning media conglomerate① for a long time. So the remaining giants ardently woo investors, trying all manner of story and seduction to win a little bit of love, to be seen as not just like all the other guys. But in this era, it's no easy task for media megaliths to find a pretty come-on to convince Wall Street of their brilliance. Sumner Redstone finally gave up and decided to slice his Viacom in half. Time Warner execs boast about a portfolio composed more or less entirely of top brands, but that pitch will go unheeded as long as it owns AOL, still the corporate equivalent of cement shoes.

The two best claims for company exceptionalism are those presented by News Corp. and Walt Disney. If I may grossly oversimplify, the stories

---

① conglomerate [kənˈglɔmərit] *n.* 集团企业

迪士尼成为赢家

正如默多克的道琼斯交易牵制了其旗下新闻集团的行动，迪士尼对媒体股票投资者迄今为止继续保持着最合理的推销辞令。

传媒大亨傲慢的呻吟早已不再时尚。 于是，残存的寡头们热情地向投资者搔首弄姿，尝试用各种各样的谎言和诱惑来赢得一点点爱意，以便看上去与所有其他的同行完全不一样。 但在这个领域，媒体巨头们要找到漂亮的诱饵，说服华尔街相信他们的辉煌，并不是一件容易的事。 萨默·雷斯顿最终选择了放弃，将他的维亚康姆公司拆分成两部分。 时代华纳的高管大肆吹嘘或多或少完全由顶级品牌组合的投资，但只要这种组合拥有美国在线，投资就无人问津，依然等同于累赘的企业。

新闻集团和迪士尼这两家公司的主张最好是另当别论。 如果用极端言简意赅的语言，我可以这样描述事情的缘由：新闻集团的鲁伯特·默多克运用他的战略才华煞费苦心地组装了一台机器，足以战胜全球媒体棋盘上的所有玩家。 迪士尼强大的品牌和无与伦比的各种赚钱方式使其获得了溢价股票估值。 它近来一直在使用"迪士尼别有洞天"的头韵标签，向投资者推销这种理念。 这两家公司去年曾遭受来自股市的冲击。 在过去的 12 个月中，迪士尼的股票下

go something like this: News Corp.'s Rupert Murdoch has employed his strategic brilliance to painstakingly assemble a machine that will outsmart all players on the global media chessboard. Disney deserves a premium stock valuation from its powerful brands and its unparalleled variety of ways to make money from them. It's been selling this notion to investors lately, under the alliterative tag "the Disney Difference." Both have been knocked around by the stock market in the past year. Disney's 27% drop over the twelve months ending recently sounds grim, but such a showing outperforms its peers and market indexes. Just compare it with News Corp.'s 57% decline. Apparently, not all exceptions are created equal.

To mangle a metaphor, Murdoch's problem is that his papers have come home to roost. His newspaper division accounted for around 19% of News Corp.'s revenue in its last fiscal year, making it the company's second-largest unit. Though there's more to Dow Jones than The Wall Street Journal, investors perceived that deal as a very expensive way to buy more newspaper assets, and time has not improved the aftertaste. A company spokesman says the company is pleased with the Journal's and Dow Jones' overall performance. And, analysts say, its TV station holdings leave News Corp. further exposed to local ad trends, which have not been encouraging. And the digital pixie dust that the MySpace purchase sprinkled over the company lost some of its power, when the

滑 27%，近期才结束了听起来很残酷的异动，但这样的表现还是超过了其他同行和市场指数。 这只是相对于新闻集团 57% 的下跌而言。 很显然，并非所有的例外都是平等的。

默多克面临的问题可以用一个令人啼笑皆非的隐喻来解释，即他的报纸产业终于自食恶果。 他的报业分部在上个财政年度占新闻集团收益的 19%，成为公司创收的第二大来源。 尽管公司的道琼斯指数比《华尔街日报》更高，但投资者认为，购入更多的报业资产是一笔昂贵的投资交易，从长线考虑不值得投资。 一位公司发言人声称，公司对《华尔街日报》和道琼斯指数的整体表现感到满意。 分析人士指出，由于公司的电视台控股脱离了新闻集团，进一步暴露在本地广告的行业动态之中，所以此举并没有增进投资者的信心。 投资"聚友网"分散了公司的主营业务，使数字仙尘技术失去了它的一些权力，公司在当时承认，管辖"聚友网"的福克斯互动传媒将会错过 10 亿美元的收入目标。 新闻集团一直没有提供本财政年度的收入目标。

一位分析人士表示，默多克"依然是这个圈子里最精明的一员。 但是这又能改变什么"？ 人们仍在继续抛售他的股票。 默多克拥有 47 亿美元的现金，据说他最近启用了两个收入来源，只买产权，也就是说，除了广告外，没有别的资金支持。

而迪士尼公司的表现可以用一个简单的例子来说明：在同等级的公司中，这个娱乐业巨头的广告收入只占总收入的很小一部分。 在广告支出遭受重挫的情况下，对你来说这或许是个好数据。 至少已经有一些投资者对迪士尼的固定卖点感兴趣，即利用产品促销、电影、主题公园等一切手段，如只要推出电影《歌舞青春》，源源不

company admitted that the Fox Interactive Media unit which houses MySpace would miss its $ 1 billion revenue target. News Corp. hasn't provided one for the fiscal year.

Murdoch is "still the smartest guy in the room, " says one analyst. "But so what? People are still selling the out of his stock." Murdoch, who's sitting on $ 4. 7 billion in cash, recently said he will only buy properties with two revenue sources — that is, nothing supported only by ads.

The explanation of Disney's performance begins with one simple fact: Among its peers, the entertainment giant derives the smallest percentage of revenues from advertising. This is a good data point to have on your side when ad spending is tanking. Disney's stated selling point — that only it can take, say, High School Musical and extrapolate① a gazillion revenue streams by leveraging everything from merchandising to movies to theme parks — has won traction with at least some investors. The mercurial reign of Michael Eisner is now in the rearview, and CEO Bob Iger wins plaudits for steadiness. The big question is what a recession — and a presumed travel slowdown — will do to Disney's theme parks business, which accounted for around a third of its revenue last quarter.

---

① extrapolate [ik'stræpəleit] *vt.* 外推

断的现金流就会收入囊中。 迈克尔·埃斯纳机智善变的统治在当下卓有成效，首席执行官鲍勃·伊格尔的稳健也赢得了大家的喝彩。最大的问题在于，经济衰退———一个假定的旅游经济放缓——将会如何影响迪士尼主题公园业务的推广。 这项业务预算占据上季度收入的三分之一。

虽然这种萧条的媒体环境只不过是若隐若现的预演，迪士尼看上去更像是比较稳妥的投资选择。 实际上，它打出的王牌依旧陈词乏力：公司较少依赖广告收入，也曾经出售过一家报刊分公司。 传媒寡头们身居高位，在宽大的办公室中郁闷地沉思，制定大胆的举措，他们也许不愿听到这一切，但在这样的时期，战略上的辉煌并不能驾驭他们的股票。 这也在一定程度上避免了股票波动对公司实体的间接影响。

知识链接 🔍

Viacom 　维亚康姆。说到国际传媒巨头，一定得提到维亚康姆。这艘传媒娱乐航空母舰在创新、推进与传播娱乐、新闻、体育和音乐方面，一直走在世界的前列。它为世界各地的广告商提供了第一大的平台，它在广播电视、户外广告和在线等领域都有不凡的表现，维亚康姆旗下拥有 CBS、MTV、尼克隆顿（Nickelodeon）、VHI、BET、派拉蒙（Paramount）、无线广播、国家广播公司（TNN）、乡村音乐电视（CMT）、娱乐时间（Showtime）、布洛克巴斯特（Blockbuster）等知名公司。《财富》杂志把维亚康姆公司的股票列为 21 世纪前 10 年中最值得购买的十大股票之一。

High School Musical 　《歌舞青春》。《歌舞青春》是迪士尼频道最成功的原

While this slow media environment is likely mere rehearsal for what looms, Disney appears to be a better bet for stability. Ultimately, its trump cards are pretty prosaic: The company is less dependent on advertising, and it sold off a newspaper division. The media moguls perched in massive offices brooding over bold moves may not want to hear it, but in times like these, strategic brilliance doesn't drive their stocks. Avoiding anything radioactive does to some extent.

(696 words)

创电视电影，它于 2006 年 1 月 20 日发行，并成功获得艾美奖。特洛伊·博尔顿和盖比瑞拉·曼提兹本是完全不同世界的两个人，一个是受父亲影响，一天到晚只顾着打篮球的篮球校队队长，另一个则是文静内向的数学天才少女。在除夕假期的一个卡拉 OK 比赛中，他俩发现原来彼此对唱歌都十分热爱，假期结束后，他们更发觉原来就读于同一学校！于是特洛伊和盖比瑞拉打算参加试音，希望成为学校最新音乐剧的男女主角。他们的朋友对此极力反对和干扰，但特洛伊和盖比瑞拉并没有放弃，反而更加积极地追寻自己的梦想，向其他同学成功地展示了他们一直隐藏起来的才华！

题　记

　　古老的欧洲文明为现代人的生活提供了源源不断的灵感，酒店式公寓就是欧洲文明为现代商务人士创造的公务出差文化模式。酒店式公寓价格相对较低，它的客户服务目标是"酒店式服务，公寓式管理"，住户不仅有独立的卧室、客厅、卫浴间、衣帽间等便利条件，还可以在厨房里自己烹饪美味的佳肴，在一天的劳顿之后蜷缩在长沙发上，面前摆几罐啤酒，惬意地观看电视中的足球比赛。酒店式公寓还为商务办公和区内员工提供打字、复印、传真、票务定购和酒店咨询等业务，人们既可以利用午餐时间做瑜伽，也可以在晚餐聚会前直接在公寓里淋浴和换衣服。舒适的家居环境和便捷的商务平台使出门在外的商务人士对酒店式公寓趋之若鹜，在紧张喧闹的工作之余享受现代生活的愉悦和快乐。

Home from Home
in a Serviced Apartment

Every week, Carole Booth, a business analyst at Shell, travels to London from Manchester on Tuesday morning and returns home on Thursday evening. Instead of staying in a hotel room, she stays in a serviced apartment.

"I've been doing it for two years," she explains. "There are a couple of reasons I prefer it. One is the size of the rooms. I have to come down to London every week and a small hotel room can become a bit like a cell. Another bonus is not having to eat out every day. I don't eat out at home every night." If nothing else, she points out, preparing her own meals prevents her putting on weight.

Ms Booth stays in accommodation at Plaza① on the River, a central London hotel that includes a number of flats, ranging from studios to double-balconied suites. Robert Claesson, the hotel general manager, describes serviced flats as "an alternative option to a hotel room — business and long-stay travellers have different needs to short- stay guests".

Indeed, when you are spending large chunks of your life away from home, life can become very inconvenient if you are confined to a hotel

---

① plaza [ˈplɑːzə] n. 广场

酒店式公寓，宾至如归

壳牌公司的业务分析师卡罗尔·布斯每周二早上从曼彻斯特出发前往伦敦，周四晚上回家。她选择了一套酒店式公寓，没有入住酒店的房间。

她解释道："两年来，我乐此不疲。我喜欢酒店式公寓有几个方面的原因。其中之一是房间的大小。我每周都必须去一趟伦敦，酒店的小房间有点像个牢房。另外一个有利的条件是我不用每天都非得外出用餐。每天晚上我都不外出吃饭。"她表示，如果没有其他的事，自己准备膳食可以防止长胖。

布斯女士的住处位于泰晤士河边的购物中心，属于伦敦市中心的一个酒店。这家酒店拥有多套公寓房，包括工作室和带有两个阳台的套房。酒店总经理罗伯特·格莱森将这种商务住宅描述为"酒店房间的另类选择，相对于短期居住的客人而言，它更能满足商务旅行者和长期停留的旅行者的特别需求"。

的确，当大量的时间消磨在家庭生活之外的地方时，如果还将自己禁锢在酒店的房间里，生活会变得很不方便。除了烹饪外，人们需要考虑自己洗衣和不在睡觉的地方工作。由于这样一些原因，当然还包括经济方面的因素，布斯女士的安排已经成为一种日益流

room. As well as cooking, there are such considerations as being able to do your own laundry and not working where you sleep. For reasons such as these — and economy — Ms Booth's arrangement is an increasingly popular one.

Cheapflights, the travel price comparison company, leases a two-bedroom apartment in the Marylebone area. "We've got a chief executive who lives in Boston," says UK general manager Francesca Ecsery, "and a lot of the US team come here regularly and stay three to five days. It's in use most of the time. It is cheaper for the company but it's so much nicer and more personal for employees, even if it is a bit less luxurious than a hotel. It's just things like having a cupboard full of biscuits."

Jo Redman, sales director at serviced apartments provider Saco, says 70 per cent of its clients are businesspeople, ranging from employees of multinationals such as Deloitte and HSBC, to smaller companies such as Aardman Animations. She, too, points to the comfort aspect: "With an apartment you can, to some extent, replicate① your lifestyle. Just things like being able to make tea, cook food from your country of origin, or crash out on the couch in front of the football with a couple of cans of lager."

For businesses, she adds, cost may be the most important consideration. "Over periods of a week or more you can drive the total cost of stay down by 20-30 per cent." And for those who really want to trim expenditure: "You can put two people from the same company in the same apartment."

"We do a lot of graduate work for banks and most graduate teams are very happy to share." In fact, she says, "sometimes recent graduates walk in and can't believe their luck". Similarly, Ms Ecsery says that

---

① replicate ['replikit] *vt.* 复制音

行的选择。

旅行比价公司"廉价飞行"在马里波恩地区出租两居室的套房。英国总经理弗朗西斯卡·瑟瑞声称："我们的客户中有一个家在波士顿的行政主管，还有许多美国团队定期到这来住 3 到 5 天。此类公寓的使用率很高。尽管它比酒店少了些许豪华，但对公司来说，租住公寓更便宜，而住户会感到更温馨，拥有更多的私人空间。它就像一个装满了饼干的橱柜。"

萨柯市商务公寓供应商的营销主管乔·瑞德曼认为，70% 的客户是商务人士，既包括德勤俱乐部和汇丰银行此类跨国公司的雇员，也有阿德曼卡通公司等小公司的员工。她还描述了商务公寓给人们提供的舒适环境："在某种程度上，拥有一套商务公寓相当于复制了你的生活方式。你好像身处自己的国家，泡茶，做饭，蜷缩在长沙发上，面前摆着几罐啤酒，舒适地观看电视中的足球比赛。"

她补充说，经商考虑得最多的是成本。"住一个星期或者更久，你可以让住宿总成本下降 20% 到 30%。"对那些真正想削减开支的人来说，"你可以将同一公司的两个人安排在同一套公寓里面"。

事实上，她认为他们"为在银行实习的毕业生做了很多工作，大部分毕业生团队很高兴分摊费用。有时你不能相信现在入住的毕业生人人都能有幸找到工作"。瑟瑞女士同样认为，费用分摊在"廉价飞行"公寓很普遍，但合租人必须受同性条件的约束。

瑞德曼女士表示，频繁入住萨柯市商务公寓的旅行者不仅有往来于纽约和伦敦两地的高管，还有悉尼和中东等其他地区的商务人士。大量承租商务公寓的公司应该为这种现象负责，因为他们实施了一个重要的变革。她指出，大大小小的公司过去倾向于经营和拥

sharing at the Cheapflights flat is very common, with the stipulation① that sharers must be of the same sex.

Ms Redman says Saco sees heavy use of such apartments by executives moving between New York and London, as well as travelers from other locations such as Sydney and the Middle East. One big change has been in the number of companies being responsible for such accommodation. In the past, she says, organizations tended to run and even own their own property but few now want to do this. "Companies don't like to have to find a handyman, vet a cleaner or buy a duvet② from John Lewis if they own one or two flats," she says.

However, says British Airways, long-stay flats are used for reasons other than comfort and cost. In some places it simply is not safe to let overseas staff rent just anywhere. "There are countries, such as Russia, where it might be necessary to have permanent accommodation in a secure compound," BA says. "Here we'd normally take a long-term lease as we always have flights going there. You basically say, that's where you're going to live."

But for those who do not have security worries, the appeal of a serviced flat remains the convenience. As Ms Ecsery points out, having an apartment near the office can be useful, even for those who do not actually need anywhere to stay. "If we're going out for an evening do, then we sometimes use it to shower and change without going home. And I've even borrowed the keys to go and do some yoga at lunchtime."

(760 words)

---

① stipulation [ˌstipjuˈleiʃən] *n.* 约束
② duvet [ˈduːvei] *n.* 羽绒被

有自己的产权,但是现在很少有人这样做。 她说:"公司如果拥有一套或两套公寓,就没有必要为雇佣杂务工、审查清洁工或是到约翰·路易斯商店买羽绒被等琐事费心了。"

但英国航空公司认为,长期租住公寓除了舒适和成本效益外,还有其他的一些原因。 在有些地方,让海外人员随处租房从根本上讲是不安全的。 英航指出:"在俄罗斯这样一些国家,也许有必要在安全住宅区拥有长期居住的处所。 我们这里通常提供长期租约,因为我们经常有去那儿的航班。 一般来说,你会认为那就是你打算入住的地方。"

对那些没有安全忧患意识的人来说,商务套房的便利条件也具有吸引力。 正如瑟瑞女士指出的,特别是对那些实际上不需要另找住宿的人来说,在办公室旁边拥有一套公寓也很实用。"如果我们打算晚间外出活动,那么我们有时候就不用回家,直接在公寓里淋浴和换衣服。 我甚至可以借用钥匙,利用午餐时间去做瑜伽。"

知识链接 🔍

Cheapflights 廉价飞行。这是一家跨国航空比价公司,在伦敦、纽约和阿姆斯特丹等地均有分公司,为客户提供美洲及欧洲廉价航空机票比价。

题　记

　　品牌是产品的"烙印"。著名品牌"可口可乐"，在美国本土每天可以卖出 1 亿瓶(杯)，若再包括 161 个国家的数字，每天就有 5 亿瓶(杯)的可口可乐出售。这种强势品牌打造的市场销售力是一个创造、存储、再创造、再存储的经营过程，它形成了 21 世纪市场营销的主流：科技品牌苹果和谷歌一直位居世界前十；零售商品牌玛莎百货和阿斯达在英国排名分列第四和第九位；中国移动成功跻身全球十大品牌的行列；高盛和微软品牌吸引了无数商学院的尖子生；星巴克在迅速拓展全球业务的同时艰难地维持着品牌初期的轰动效应；麦当劳冲破全球美国化的限制，排名直线上升。强大的品牌效应就像空气一样无处不在，它们抢占市场份额，承担投资风险，引导消费潮流，提升了企业的综合实力。

Strong Names Beat the Market

Branding is becoming ever more important as companies face an increasingly global and competitive marketplace. Millward Brown Optimor's third annual ranking of the world's top 100 most powerful brands is based partly on WPP's Brandz database, which covers more than 50,000 of them. It found that the world's top 100 brands have a total value of about $ 1,900bn, equivalent to the GDP of Italy.

"Brand is becoming more and more important," says Joanna Seddon, chief executive of Millward Brown Optimor. "Technology brands have done very well this year, Google and Apple are in the top 10. For the second year running Google is the world's most valuable brand. Some of the world's most successful companies are successful because they built their brand along with the business. Orange is a good example of that. They invested in the brand before they even had a business."

But Millward Brown Optimor has also been measuring the effects of brand on stock market performance — an area where little research has been done. It has created a "Brandz" portfolio① incorporating all the

---

① portfolio [pɔːtˈfəuljəu] *n.* 证券投资组合

顶级品牌战胜市场

　　在公司面临市场全球化和竞争白热化之际，品牌也成为越来越重要的标志。明略行咨询公司根据环球网"品牌"数据库提供的部分数据，对世界最具影响力的百强企业品牌进行了第三次年度排名。这个"品牌"数据库覆盖了 5 万多个品牌。明略行咨询公司发现，世界百强企业品牌的总价值达 1.9 万亿美元，相当于意大利的年度国内生产总值。

　　明略行咨询公司的总裁乔安娜·塞顿认为，"品牌正变得越来越重要。科技品牌在今年发挥非常出色，谷歌和苹果都位居前 10 位。在下个年度的经营中，谷歌是世界上最有价值的品牌。世界上有些非常成功的公司，其成功的原因就在于他们建立了相关的商业品牌。橙色公司就是很好的例子。他们甚至在成立公司之前就投资创建了品牌"。

　　明略行咨询公司还测算了品牌效应在股票市场的表现，这是一个人们很少涉及的研究领域。它创造了一个"品牌"投资组合，并把所有可能投资的前百强品牌融入其中。品牌必须是拥有流动股份的股份有限公司。如果投资组合的收益用美元计算，结果就容易受货币的影响。品牌投资组合以标准普尔 500 指数为参照，因为这个

brands in its top 100 survey that it was possible to invest in. The brands had to be public limited companies with liquid stock. The portfolio returns were measured in US dollars so the results are subject to currency effects. The Brandz portfolio is benchmarked against the S&P 500 as this exchange mirrors its composition most closely — large and small caps, industry and inter-national exposure. "We didn't use the FTSE, as eight of the world's top brands are in the US so it would be skewed① by currency effects, " says Malte Nuhn, senior consultant at Millward Brown Optimor.

Not all companies received equal investment at the onset of the portfolio. There was a higher investment in companies with stronger brands and those whose branded businesses were a larger part of the group. Millward Brown also isolated the stronger brands into a separate portfolio — those that have a brand contribution above 30 per cent in the rankings the brand contributions are indexed but in fact they are percentages. This "Strong Brands" portfolio incorporates around two-thirds of the world's top 100 brands. The S&P had risen 3 per cent over 12 months, the Brandz Top 100 portfolio was up 15 per cent and the strong brands portfolio was up 22 per cent.

The Millward Brown study showed that products and companies with strong brand value enjoyed markedly stronger returns in good times and also during the recent market downturn. Hayes Roth, chief marketing officer of Landor Associates, the consultancy, says: "There is remarkable

---

① skew [skju:] *adj.* 歪曲的

指数与该组合的构成最接近，包括大型股和小型股的比例、行业和国别构成等。 明略行咨询公司的高级咨询师马尔特·努恩表示："我们没有使用富时指数，因为世界顶级品牌中有 8 个在美国，如果参照富时指数，可能会受到汇率变化的扭曲。"

并不是所有的公司在投资组合起步时都能收到相同的投资额。品牌效应较强、品牌业务占据公司较大部分的企业，获得的投资额度较高。 明略行咨询公司还抽出一些较强的品牌，即品牌贡献率达到 30% 的品牌，构成单独的投资组合。 在排名中，品牌贡献率用指数表示；但实际上，它们以百分数来表示。 这种"强势品牌"组合涵盖了世界百强品牌中的三分之二。 在过去的 12 个月中，标准普尔上升了 3%，前百强的品牌投资组合上升了 15%，而强势的品牌投资组合则上升了 22%。

明略行咨询公司的研究显示，无论是在牛市还是在最近的市场低迷时期，具有强大品牌价值的公司和产品能明显获得较高的回报。 朗涛策略设计顾问公司的首席营销官海斯·罗思表示："强大的品牌价值和强劲的股票表现之间存在着显著的一致性。 品牌力量与股市表现紧密相连，平均来说，品牌价值可以为一个公司增加逾25% 的市值——具体数字可能因公司类型而有所不同。"塞顿女士认为，这种超额收益后的驱动力包含着这样的事实：强大的品牌可以更容易地增加他们的收入和市场份额。 这是因为这样的产品更有吸引力，人们更愿意拥趸这些产品。 努恩先生补充道："你也有可能获得溢价。 苹果产品的售价比竞争对手的同类产品高出约 20%，这会影响利润率。"

consistency between strong brand value and stock performance. Brand power can be significantly linked to stock market strength, adding on average — and depending on category — more than 25 per cent market value to an organization." Ms Seddon believes that the drivers behind this outperformance include the fact that strong brands can more readily increase their revenues and market share. This is because people are more attracted to the products and are more likely to be loyal to them. "You also may have the possibility of achieving a price premium," adds Mr. Nuhn. "Apple's products sell for roughly 20 per cent more than equivalents from rivals, which will affect margins."

But there are plenty of examples of strong brands hitting nasty bumps in the road. "Look at Starbucks. You can do a world class job of building brands and do everything right but when you rapidly expand your global footprint it is hard to maintain what made the brand great in the first place. They over-extended themselves," says Mr. Roth. "McDonald's suffered with the Americanization of the world but they went back and reinvented themselves and they have moved up the list," he adds.

Studies have shown that a strong brand affects not only demand but also the supply chain. For example, if you have a strong brand such as Goldman Sachs or Microsoft it is easier to attract top graduates from business schools. "You can pay them less and they will stay longer, you can get better terms with suppliers. If you have a strong brand and invest in new products or markets you can get somebody else to take your investment risk," says Ms Seddon.

但是，也有很多大品牌摔跟头、一蹶不起的例子。罗斯先生说："看看星巴克。创建品牌时，你能干得不错，什么事都做得很对，但当你迅速拓展全球业务时，很难维持品牌初期的轰动效应。这种症结就是自我扩张过度。"罗斯补充说："麦当劳起初受全球美国化的限制，但是他们回到原点，彻底改造自己，他们已经在排名上直线上升。"

研究表明，强劲的品牌不仅影响需求，也同样影响供给链。例如，如果你拥有高盛或微软这样的大牌，吸引商学院的尖子生就容易得多。塞顿女士认为，"即使你支付较低的薪水，在相当一段时间内，他们也不会离开公司。你还可以从供应商那儿得到更优惠的条件。如果你有一个强大的品牌，在新产品或市场投资时，可以让别人替你承担投资风险"。

虽然明略行咨询公司认为它的研究已经引起了基金管理机构的广泛兴趣，但迄今为止尚未出现全球品牌基金。这些基金管理机构提出了建立全球品牌基金的理念，以数据为基础挑选股票。罗斯先生说："看看明略行的研究。如果你已经挑选了前五名，那么就没什么大问题了。对于前百强的品牌来说，由于存在可能会影响业绩的其他因素，免不了经历许多大起大落的博弈。但是，强大的品牌会让你预见未来，助你取得更好的名次。全球品牌基金将是一个长期的投资，它应该看起来像个蓝筹股基金。如果有这样一个基金，应该会很棒。当然会有大量的收益。"

中国品牌不断壮大的同时，美国品牌仍然在行业称霸。美国品牌的强势在北美十大品牌排行榜中雄踞榜首，有八个进入全球排名

There are no global brand funds to date, although Millward Brown Optimor says its study has generated a lot of interest from the fund management community who have mooted① the idea of creating a global brand fund where they would use the data as a basis for stock picking. Mr. Roth says: "Look at the Optimor study. If you had picked the top five you would have done OK. Of the top 100 brands there is a lot of jockeying② up and down because there are other things that affect performance. But strong brands will see you through and leave you in a far better place. A global brand fund would be a long-haul investment, it ought to look like a blue chip fund. It would be terrific to see. There is certainly a lot of interest."

US brands still rule the roost as China marches on. The strength of US brands is underlined by the North American Top 10, which shares eight brands with the top 10 in the global rankings. Only the two leading brands in Asia and Europe, China Mobile and Nokia respectively, make it into the global top 10. The two extra brands in the North American ranking are Wal-Mart, which fell out of the global top 10 but is still 13th overall, and Bank of America, which slipped one place in the Top 100, to 14th, but had the consolation of seeing its main rival Citi fall seven places, to 15th.

China Mobile and the three Chinese banks in the Asian Top 10 —

---

① moot [muːt] vt. 提出
② jockey ['dʒɔki] vi. 瞒,欺骗

前十。 仅有的另外两个领先的品牌在亚洲和欧洲，分别是中国移动和诺基亚，他们也成功跻身全球十大品牌的行列。 沃尔玛和美国银行是北美另外两大排名靠前的品牌。 沃尔玛虽然退出全球排名前十，但总排名仍然位居第十三位。 美国银行在前百强中的位置下降了一个名次，排名第十四位，但令它欣慰的是，其竞争对手花旗银行下降了七个名次，排名第十五位。

中国移动和中国工商银行、中国建设银行以及中国银行等三家中国银行位居亚洲品牌前十。 他们的品牌价值实现了大幅提升。而其他亚洲公司的绩效却微乎其微，三星公司的品牌价值甚至下降了 7% 。 与日本、韩国及香港地区相比，这种差异强调了这样一个事实，即中国内地的发展势头更为强劲。

在欧洲，沃达丰的品牌价值上升了 75% ，达到了现在的 370 亿美元，确保其在地区排名中上升到第二，位于全球百强的第十一名，排名上升了十一个名次。 保时捷的品牌价值激增了 62% ，在地区前十中排位第六，在全球百强中升至第二十八位，提升了十二个名次。 特斯科在全球百强排名中上升了七个名次，跃居第二十五位，它同样也是欧洲第五大、英国第二大的最具影响力的品牌，价值为 232 亿美元。 另外两家零售商——玛莎百货和阿斯达——在英国排名分列第四和第九位。

知识链接 🔍

Millward Brown Optimor 明略行咨询公司是一家全球领先的市场咨询机

ICBC, China Construction Bank and Bank of China — all achieved big rises in their brand value, whereas the gains at the other Asian companies were much more modest, and Samsung even suffered a 7 per cent fall. The disparity① emphasizes the stronger dynamics of mainland China as compared with Japan, South Korea and Hong Kong.

In Europe, Vodafone's 75 per cent rise in brand value, to $ 37bn, takes it to second place in the regional ranking and up 11 places to 11th in the global 100. Porsche's 62 per cent surge in brand value takes it to sixth spot in the regional top 10, and 12 places up the global top 100 to 28th. Tesco, up seven places to 25th in the top 100, is the fifth most powerful European brand with a value of $ 23.2bn, and second strongest UK brand. Two other retailers, Marks & Spencer and Asda, come fourth and ninth respectively in the UK ranking.

(1,159 words)

---

① disparity [dis'pæriti] n. 不一致

构，它致力于为客户提供拥有广阔视角的解决方案，以及专业的咨询建议。明略行咨询公司在 44 个国家拥有 76 家分公司，并为全球百强企业中的 90% 的企业提供服务。

WPP　环球网存在提供器（WPP WebPresenceProvider）。

题　记

　　"空中飞人"大部分时间是在飞机的商务舱上度过的，他们随时可能出现在世界的任何地方。这类人群通常是大企业的决策者、高层代表、业务主管等，他们的业务遍布世界各地。为了吸引"空中飞人"，旅游供应商提供了越来越多的廉价服务。英国航空公司为购买国内航线全价票的人士提供一次免费的希思罗机场和盖特威克快车返程火车票；俄罗斯洲际航空公司为了刺激那些喜欢讨价还价的旅游公司，削减了高达 5% 的票价；维京大西洋航空公司开创了豪华经济客舱，使乘客享有与商务舱同样的服务；澳航为爱好各异的旅客提供个性化的服务，除满足他们的需求之外，还通过累积一定数量的里程给商务人士提供免票或升舱等奖励。公司逐渐放低姿态，以软化的方式招揽旅客，但他们所做的一切都是为了保持公司的收支平衡，从供给方市场向需求方市场转化。

Wooing the Corporate Flyer

As someone who travels once a month on business, David Solomons, chief executive of Culture Smart Consulting, has a particular predilection① for bonus airline miles. These days, though, he can choose from any number of incentives for travel. "There are so many inducements coming in the post now from travel suppliers, " he says.

The economic downturn is prompting travel providers to offer a growing range of frills② for business travelers. The UK hotel group Malmaison and Hotel du Vin has already begun price-led promotions. "We have flexible room rates and we're nimble on our feet, " says Robert Cook, chief executive. Such incentives are important: corporate travel provides the bulk of profits for airlines, hotels and car hire companies.

British Airways is one airline offering promotions to cement loyalty. "In a typical year we do all sorts of things, but with travel managers having to make budgets go further we've created promotions that save cost to the company, " says Richard Tams, general manager, UK and global corporate sales. "It's a different accent this year; we're trying to upweight the cost element to the corporate and give them more bang for their

---

① predilection [ˌpriːdiˈlekʃən] *n.* 偏爱
② frill [fril] *n.* 虚饰

吸引公司飞人

文化管理咨询公司的总裁大卫·所罗门每月有一次例行的公务旅行，他是个特别偏爱航空里程奖励的人。不过，他近期可以参加任意选择航班的促销活动。他说："现在有很多诱惑，旅游服务供应商们不停地以邮件的形式促销。"

经济不景气促使旅游供应商为商务旅行者提供越来越多的超值服务。英国酒店集团马尔梅森已经开始了以价格为主导的促销活动。首席执行官罗伯特·库克声称："我们的房价可以上下浮动，我们的安排灵活机动。"这些刺激很重要，因为商务旅行为航空公司、酒店和汽车租赁公司带来了丰厚的利润。

英航是一家用促销来增强消费者忠诚度的航空公司。英航的英国及全球销售总经理理查德·泰姆斯说："典型情况下，我们每年都要承接各种各样的任务，但对那些要做进一步预算的差旅经理，我们采取了一些促销活动，以帮助公司节省开支。但今年的重点不同。我们努力提高公司的成本比重，给他们的消费更多的回报。"

在英国，购买英航国内航线全价票的公司职员可享受一次免费的希思罗机场和盖特威克快车返程火车票，英航的普通旅客则可享受特定路线的双倍里程促销服务。这是一个全球性的促销计划：例

buck."

In the UK, BA is offering a free Heathrow and Gatwick Express return train ticket when companies buy a full-fare domestic flight, and to the traveler it is offering route-specific double miles promotions. It is a worldwide scheme: in the US, for example, it is offering London-bound travelers two free hotel nights in three- and four-star properties linked to discounted fares. One airline, the Russian Transaero, opted for fare cuts of up to 5 per cent to reflect the fall in the price of oil.

Such concessions are spurring many businesses to bargain with travel companies. "We're asking all our supplier base for more discounts," says Jan Tucker-Jones, business travel manager of BT. One hotel group, InterContinental Hotels, has offered BT discounts on food and beverages at its properties worldwide. "We will push more business their way. It shows commitment to us," Ms Tucker-Jones says.

"Premium economy①" is an increasingly popular option. Many cost- conscious employers are trading down to such flights during the day and restricting employees' use of business class to overnight flights between the US and UK, for example. On Virgin Atlantic, which pioneered the premium economy cabin, passengers enjoy some of the same frills they would be used to in business, such as dedicated check-in, cabin crew and menu and laptop power at every seat. Legroom is not as generous as in business class but is still up to 6in more than the squash in economy class. Qantas is the latest airline to join the fray, introducing premium economy across its 747 fleet this spring. And when the new addition to its fleet, the double-decker Airbus A380, takes to the air it will raise the bar still more. Premium economy passengers will then enjoy extras such as a self-service

---

① Premium economy 豪华经济舱

如，从美国飞抵伦敦的乘客可以享受折扣服务，在三星级酒店或四星级酒店免费住宿两晚。俄罗斯洲际航空公司则因为油价下降，削减了高达 5% 的票价。

旅游供应商的让价引起了许多企业与旅游公司之间的讨价还价。英国电信的商务旅行经理扬塔克·琼斯主张："我们要求所有的供应商提供更多的折扣。"英国电信可以享受洲际酒店集团全球连锁店的饮食和酒水折扣。塔克·琼斯说："我们给他们带来了更多的生意。这是他们对我们的承诺。"

"豪华经济舱"受到越来越多的商务人士的青睐。许多成本意识强烈的雇主限制员工乘坐白天航班和商务舱，例如，他们要求员工乘坐往返于美国和英国之间的夜间航班。英国维京航空公司最先引进了豪华经济客舱。豪华经济客舱的乘客享有与商务舱乘客同等的服务，如专用登机手续办理、航班空服人员、专业的菜单，每个座位上提供笔记本电脑电源等。虽然供伸腿的空间没有商务舱大，但仍然比拥挤的经济舱大 6 英寸。澳航是新近加入竞争的航空公司，今年春天在其 747 机上引进了豪华经济舱。当豪华经济舱投入使用时，双层空客 A380 推出了酒吧服务。豪华经济舱的乘客将享受额外服务，例如自助服务酒吧、增加两英寸的席位以及装在每个座位上的 USB 接口。

陆地仍然是商务旅行竞争的主战场，但即使在这里也有便宜的项目。例如，往返于伦敦市中心或金丝雀码头和希思罗机场的 Dot2Dot 专线配备九座奔驰商务车，单程只需 20 英镑（约 36 美元，25 欧元）。在英国，雇主不能减少其雇员的福利以降低成本。公司过失杀人法案意味着企业有责任保证旅客的人身安全。新法令规

bar, 2in more seat pitch and USB ports at each seat.

But much of the stress of travelling is on the ground and even here there are bargains. The Dot2Dot shuttle between central London or Canary Wharf and Heathrow, for example, offers a ride in a shared nine-seater Mercedes shuttle from £20 ($36, €25) one way. In the UK, employers cannot afford to cut costs by scrimping① on their employees' wellbeing. The Corporate Manslaughter & Homicide Bill means companies have a duty of care to keep their travelers safe. The new act does not have to prove individual failure, so a company can be charged. Employers must, for example, ensure their travelers are well informed about their destination, that the hotel they stay in is in a safe part of the city and convenient for business meetings, and that it looks after their down time. Hoteliers already commonly offer multiple restaurants, gyms, spas and bars. The oil and gas operator BG Group has set gold standards in this regard, with a wide range of provision, such as a car to get home safely after flights of more than seven hours' duration or after overtime, flight safety awareness training, twice-yearly checks on any private car used for business and mandating that travelers attend half-day defensive driving courses.

"The corporate world has gradually softened its approach to travelers," says Tom Stone, director of Sirius Management, a business travel consultancy. "But it's all to do with balance: the company can't go out of business."

(744 words)

---

① scrimp [skrimp] vi. 缩减

定，乘客无需证明单个人的失职就能起诉一家公司。 例如，雇主必须确保旅客熟悉目的地，确保旅客入住的酒店位于城市的安全地带，并且方便旅客在此召开商务会议，还要考虑旅客的下机时间。酒店通常会提供各类餐厅、健身房、温泉浴场和酒吧。 石油和天然气运营商英国天然气集团在这方面已经设立了大量的黄金标准，如果旅客飞行超过 7 小时或乘机时间延长，会安排汽车送他们安全抵家。 这些黄金标准还包括飞行安全意识培训、每年检测两次用于商务的私家车以及要求旅客参加为期半天的防御性驾驶课程。

天狼星商务旅游顾问公司的经理汤姆·斯通说："公司逐渐放低姿态来招揽旅客。 但所做的一切都是为了保持收支平衡：公司不可能倒闭。"

知识链接 🔍

British Telecom （BT）英国电信是英国最大电信设施硬件的营运者，在全球 170 个国家设有营业点或办事处，海外营业处的营业额占集团总营业额的三分之一。

BG Group 英国天然气集团是英国最大的综合性能源公司之一，它集气源勘探、开采和国际市场开发为一体，与各级政府、部门和相关单位紧密合作，致力于引领整个天然气的产业链，充当天然气勘探、生产、运输、配送和供应的行业先锋。英国天然气集团的资本总额超过 480 亿美元，业务遍及五大洲 25 个国家。

题　记

　　品牌的认知度对任何公司都极其重要。要创建一个真正有影响力的品牌，产品和消费者之间需要建立一种归属感、友谊和信赖感。品牌归属感是消费者品牌忠诚度培育规划试图催生的结果，是品牌体现出来的某些东西和消费者心里所需要的某些东西产生的强烈共鸣，就像美国世界级的滑雪胜地陶谷，其令人难以置信的地形和独特的地域文化，吸引了无数滑雪的忠实爱好者。品牌友谊是产生信任感的基础，品牌经营者可以采取措施倡导友谊，并确认自己也正在尽职尽责，就像很多人早上必到星巴克喝咖啡一样，与其说是去品尝咖啡，还不如说是去拜访一个值得信任的、熟悉的老朋友。品牌信赖感取决于良好的品牌承诺，它需要时间在品牌与客户之间建立强烈的感情纽带，就像在异地他乡偶然发现汉堡王时，你会觉得世界是如此美好！

How to Build Brand Friendship

Human beings are social creatures. We need interaction with one another. It's the way we're made. When we meet someone new, we tend either to be drawn to them or to be disinterested for a whole host of reasons, some of which we may not even realize. Over time, however, we develop a continually evolving stable of relationships, some of which last for a lifetime.

That human dynamic is the root of brand loyalty as well. Our "relationships" with brands aren't nearly as deep or meaningful as human relationships, but they do share some of the same characteristics. The extent to which you can create a sense of belonging, friendship, and dependability between your brand and customers is the extent to which you have a powerful brand asset.

Belonging

We are all members of different clubs. Our family is a club, our church is a club, and our place of employment is even a club. In some sense we "belong" to each of these clubs by choice — we choose whom to marry, where to worship, and where to work because we identify

如何建立品牌友谊

　　人是一种社会动物。 我们需要相互交流。 这是我们生存的方式。 当我们碰到陌生的面孔时，也许我们会变得很亲近，也许由于种种原因我们根本就对对方不感兴趣，有些原因我们可能根本意识不到。 然而，随着时间的流逝，我们逐渐形成了稳定的人际关系，有些关系伴随人的一生。

　　人类的这种活力也是品牌忠诚度的根源所在。 我们和品牌之间的"关系"虽然远不如人际关系那样富有深意和内涵，但是两者确实有很多共同之处。 你所建立的品牌与消费者之间的归属感、友谊和可靠性相互联系的程度越深，你的品牌价值就越强大。

归属感

　　我们都是不同社团中的成员。 我们的家庭是一个社团，我们的教堂是一个社团，甚至连我们工作的地方也可以称之为社团。 在某种意义上，我们自愿"属于"这些社团中的一员——我们选择与谁结婚，去哪里做礼拜，以及选择在什么地方工作，因为我们以某种形式和方式视他们为同一类人。 前不久我到东海岸的时候，碰到一个游客穿着我以前所在高中的 T 恤衫。 我很自然地和她攀谈起来，仿佛我们属于同一个社团。

with the people in them in some form or fashion. I was on the East Coast recently and saw a tourist sporting a sweatshirt from my high school across the country. I quite naturally struck up a conversation with her, as we were part of the same club.

Few people have a choice of where they go to high school, but as we get older our affiliations are increasingly a matter of preference. For example, I am a "Pepper." As a self-identified member of the Dr Pepper fraternity, I have an understanding of the brand that runs deep. I actually think the management at Dr Pepper has never really understood what the brand means to fans like me. If you're a Pepper east of the Mississippi where the drink is scarce, you know what I mean.

Auto brands generate a great sense of belonging as well. Ever spoken to a BMW enthusiast about his loyalty to the brand? It's powerful. Saturn (GM) and Volkswagen are two other automakers that have historically done a good job of creating a sense of belonging around their brands. So has Harley-Davidson with its Harley Owners Group. You're either in it, or you're very definitely not.

Cosmetics can also generate a strong sense of identification, as Avon and Mary Kay loyalists can attest. So does Taos Ski Valley, a world-class destination that, because of its fabulous terrain and unique local culture, has attracted an incredible following of loyalists.

What drives this sense of belonging? Arguably the most important factor in branding: relevance. Brands that generate the strongest sense of tribal identity are so relevant to the wants and needs of their customers

很少有人能够选择上哪所高中，但是随着年龄的增长，我们的社团关系越来越显现出仁者见仁、智者见智的状态。 比如说，我是个"胡椒"粉丝，作为一名自我认同的"胡椒博士"兄弟联谊会的成员，我对这个品牌有着深刻的理解。 实际上，我认为"胡椒博士"的管理层从未真正意识到这个品牌对我这样的粉丝意味着什么。 这种饮料在密西西比河东并不常见，如果你是当地的"胡椒"粉丝，应该明白我的意思。

汽车品牌同样会给人强烈的归属感。 你曾经和宝马汽车的狂热爱好者谈及过他对这个品牌的热爱吗？ 他肯定会说爱得发狂。 土星（通用汽车公司旗下的品牌）和大众汽车是另外两家汽车制造商，他们在历史上曾经给品牌创造了一种归属感，并取得了不错的成效。 哈雷-戴维森公司的哈雷车友俱乐部也同样如此。 你要么对这种品牌痴迷，要么彻底地嗤之以鼻。

化妆品也同样能产生一种强烈的品牌认同感，雅芳和玫凯琳品牌的忠实用户可以作证。 美国世界级的滑雪胜地陶谷，因其令人难以置信的地形和独特的地域文化，吸引了无数滑雪的忠实爱好者。

这种归属感是如何产生的呢？ 可以说，最关键的因素就是品牌的相关度。 品牌体现出来的某些东西和消费者心底所需要的某些东西产生强烈的共鸣，这就是消费者品牌忠诚度培育规划试图催生的结果，但是你不可能花钱买来这种归属感。 就像某人买了电影票你就让他看电影一样。

友谊

20 世纪 70 年代创建堪萨斯摇滚乐队的天才克里·利乌格瑞恩的

that they generate a natural gravitational pull. This is what customer loyalty programs attempt to generate, but you can't buy a sense of belonging. It's like offering to take someone to the movies if they purchase your ticket.

Friendship

Kerry Livgren, the creative genius behind the 1970s rock 'n' roll band Kansas, said it simply, and perhaps best: "The only way to have a friend is to be one." The great brands understand this. Starbucks has been picked on a lot lately, but it wouldn't be on such a pedestal① if it didn't do a terrific job of making friends with its customers. For many people, their morning appointment with Starbucks is like visiting with a trusted old friend — familiar and comfortable.

I travel a lot, and whenever I take a morning flight out of the beautiful Albuquerque Sunport I grab a breakfast burrito from the La Hacienda kiosk inside security. Do I think about my "friendship" with this brand every time? Not at all. But whenever I go to the airport, I enjoy the familiar taste and friendly people behind the counter.

I feel the same way about my running shoes. I'm not a serious runner by any means, but I have tried a lot of different shoe brands over the years, and when I pull my trusted Avias out of the closet I know they'll do their part, as any friend would. The same is true of the little sandwich shop on the main drag in Cuba, N.M., where I take my kids to chop

---

① pedestal ['pedistl] *n.* 基础

一句话也许简单，但是最好的诠释。 他说："交友的唯一方式就是自己够朋友。"大品牌深谙此道。 星巴克最近的客流量很大，这是因为星巴克在与顾客交友方面做了非常了不起的工作，否则不会出现这种支持率。 对很多人来说，早上到星巴克喝咖啡就像拜访一个值得信赖的老朋友——熟悉而舒适。

我经常旅行，无论何时，当我乘早上的航班飞离美丽的阿尔伯克基机场时，我都会在安全门内的庄园亭小卖部买一个它的墨西哥玉米煎饼当早餐。 我会像惦记"朋友"那样每时每刻都记着那个品牌吗？ 完全不会。 但是无论什么时候我去机场，我都喜欢那种熟悉的味道以及柜台后面那些友善的人。

我对运动鞋也有同样的感觉。 我并不是一名虔诚的跑步爱好者，但这些年来，我买过很多不同品牌的鞋子，每当我从鞋柜里拿出心爱的阿瓦斯品牌时，我就知道他们会像任何朋友一样尽自己的一份力量。 当我每年带着孩子们去挖圣诞树的时候，都会经过一家位于新墨西哥州古巴主干道边卖三明治的小店，那里同样能够找到亲切的感觉。 这些品牌多年来一直是我的好朋友，它们现在几乎轻而易举就能赚到我的钱。

如同与人类的朋友相处，我们采用的品牌给了自己一种舒适和熟悉的感觉。 我们对这些品牌逐渐了解，并产生了信任感，有意无意地抵制竞争性的"陌生"品牌。 我们选择的品牌通过连续性，即品牌的另一基本特征，赢得了我们的信任。 这就提出了一个重要观点：你不可能通过强制手段得到友谊。 作为一个经营者，强迫人们对你的品牌产生好感是不现实的。 但是，你可以采取措施倡导友谊，并确认你也正在尽职尽责。

down our Christmas tree every year. These brands have been such good friends over the years that they now get my business almost without asking.

As with human friends, the brands we adopt as our own give us a sense of comfort and familiarity; we've come to know and trust them as opposed to the "stranger" that a competing brand represents intentionally or unintentionally. Our chosen brands have earned our trust through another essential aspect of branding: consistency, which brings up an important point — you can't force friendship. As a marketer, there's no way to compel people to feel comfortable with your brand. You can, however, take steps to initiate friendship and make sure that you're doing your part.

Dependability

Friendships that aren't stable aren't really friendships. Sure, all relationships have their ups and downs, but one of the definitions of a true friend is someone you can count on. In the same way, brands that prove themselves dependable over time win our loyalty. Remember the old saying, "No one ever got fired for buying IBM." The truth of that statement was rooted in IBM's reputation for dependability. IBM may have been expensive, but it was dependable, and that was important.

Sometimes dependability manifests itself in surprising ways. Years ago my wife and I enjoyed a vacation in Jamaica. It's a beautiful island with beautiful people and wonderful food. But if you've ever spent much time in Jamaica you can get a little tired of allspice, a flavor that tends to dominate much of the cuisine. Imagine my delight on one of our

信赖感

不牢固的友谊不是真正的友谊。 当然，所有关系都有自身的起伏，但是真正的朋友是你可以依靠的人，这是朋友的定义之一。 同样，随着时间的流逝被证明是可靠的品牌赢得了我们的信赖。 记得有一句老话："没有人会因为买 IBM 而被开除。"这句话道出了一个事实，那就是 IBM 可靠的声誉深入人心。 IBM 在价格方面可能有点贵，但是它值得信赖，这才是重要的。

信赖感有时以一种让人感到惊讶的方式出现。 许多年前我和妻子到牙买加度假。 那是一座美丽的岛屿——美丽的人民，美味的食物。 但是，如果你在牙买加待得太久，就会对那儿的多香果粉有点厌烦，因为这种香料往往主导了大部分的菜肴。 可以想象我们在异地他乡偶然发现汉堡王时的高兴劲。 我知道，我在世界上的任何地方都可以吃到熟悉的、可信赖的汉堡。

建立信赖感需要时间。 正如人与人之间的关系一样，品牌需要时间与客户建立强烈的感情纽带。 冲动令人兴奋，这一点是那些深夜商业信息广告的基础，但是冲动不可能持久。 举棋不定，还是依附于品牌，取决于如何交付良好的品牌承诺。

想想那些最知名的品牌：西南航空公司、苹果公司、易趣公司、卡特彼勒公司。 他们了解归属感、友谊和信赖感的原则，采取相应的策略对待客户。 他们明白这些原则代表着什么，所以总是努力克制自己，避免过分追求商业利益，因为这会损害来之不易的忠诚度。 其实你也可以做到，你这样做得越多，公司在将来的某一天与那些知名公司同日而语的可能性就越大。

excursions when we spotted a Burger King. I knew that no matter where in the world I was I could step up to that counter and get a familiar, dependable Whopper.

Dependability requires time. Just as it does with human relationships, it takes time for brands to develop strong bonds with their customers. Infatuation① is exciting (the basis for those late-night infomercials), but infatuation never lasts. It turns into either ambivalence② or attachment depending upon how well the brand promise is delivered.

Think about the strongest brands out there: Southwest Airlines, Apple, eBay, even Caterpillar. They understand the principles of belonging, friendship, and dependability, and they treat their customers accordingly. They know what they stand for and refrain from chasing business that would compromise their hard-won loyalty. You can, too, and the more you do so the greater the likelihood your company may one day be mentioned in the same breath as they are.

(1,136 words)

---

① infatuation [inˌfætjʊˈeiʃən] *n.* 迷恋
② ambivalence [æmˈbiveiləns] *n.* 正反感情并存

知识链接

Dr Pepper 中文名称常译作：胡椒博士、莘芨博士、乐倍、澎泉等，是美国 Dr Pepper/Seven Up(七喜)公司生产的一种焦糖碳酸饮料，该公司作为吉百利史威士公司的一个分支，坐落于得克萨斯州达拉斯市区。"胡椒博士"创立于 19 世纪 80 年代，是一种用墨西哥菝葜制作的特殊果汁混合物，最常见的有胡椒博士原味、胡椒博士健怡口味、胡椒博士樱桃味等。这种清凉饮料凭借其褒贬不一的独特口味在全球拥有一大批忠实的粉丝。

题　记

对所有的天才参与者及丰厚的奖金回报而言，美国崭新的金融体系在市场的检验下一败涂地。鉴于这种情况，美国中央银行行长保罗·沃尔克提出了从根本上重新考虑金融监管机制的主要原则。第一，将所有超过一定规模的杠杆机构置于监管之下，形成完整的监管覆盖面。第二，运用权益资本对金融体系发起缓冲，以此应对任何特定类别的风险。第三，在博弈中蜕变，要求贷款人持有部分证券贷款的股权。第四，机构在萧条期的最低注册资本应该只迎合扩张期的更高目标水平。第五，增强信息透明度。第六，坚持所有的衍生品在交易所完成交易。第七，调整激励措施。即使监管永远呈高度不完美的状态，金融市场的有序运行仍然是国家与公众的期盼。

Seven Principles
of Finance Regulation

"Simply stated, the bright new financial system—for all its talented participants, for all its rich rewards — has failed the test of the market place." Paul Volcker.

Paul Volcker is the giant among contemporary central bankers, both literally and figuratively. He it was who had the moral courage to crush inflation as chairman of the Federal Reserve between 1979 and 1987. When Mr. Volcker speaks, people listen. What he had to tell the economic club of New York last month was well worth listening to. His summation was so devastating, because so true.

Mr. Volcker noted that this crisis is not unique. On the contrary, "today's financial crisis is the culmination, as I count them, of at least five serious breakdowns of systemic significance in the past 25 years — on the average one every five years. Warning enough that something rather basic is amiss." Those who do not heed such warnings are fated to suffer something yet worse. So what is to be done? There is a part of me — quite a large part, in fact — that says: "Forget regulation: it will never work. Apart from normal laws against fraud, let the financial system live and die by the laws of competitive markets. If businesses fail, let them simply go down, with all their shareholders, customers and employees.

金融监管的七条原则

　　"简单地说，对所有的天才参与者及丰厚的奖金回报而言，崭新的金融体系在市场的检验下一败涂地。"保罗·沃尔克如是说。

　　保罗·沃尔克是当代一位卓越的中央银行行长，这个头衔名副其实。　保罗·沃尔克还是一身正气的美联储主席，他粉碎了1979年至1987年的通货膨胀。　沃尔克先生任何时候发表演说都会引起大家的关注。　他上个月在纽约经济俱乐部的讲话就很值得一听。他的总结因为太过真实而令人如此震惊。

　　沃尔克先生指出，这场危机无独有偶。　恰恰相反，"如我所言，今天的金融危机是过去25年中至少五次严重的制度性经济衰退的高潮——平均每5年一次。　我们需要发出足够的警告：有些相当基本的东西出差错了"。　谁不听从警告，谁就注定要面对越来越糟糕的状况。　应该做些什么？　我的职责告诉我，事实上有相当大的一部分职责应该是"忘记规则，因为它从来不起作用。　除去防止欺诈行为的通行法律，让市场竞争法则来决定金融体系的生死。　如果企业倒闭，应该顺其自然，所有的股东、客户和员工也不例外。　与此同时，我们会提醒用户关注持续不断的危险"。　我猜想，这种方式可能让我们拥有比今天更好的金融系统。　但是，正如北岩银行和

Meanwhile, we will remind users constantly of the dangers." I suspect this approach might give us a better financial system than the one we have today. But it is one we cannot have because governments will not dare let us, as experience with Northern Rock and Bear Stearns has reminded us. The public, governments feel, must be protected from banks and banks must be protected from themselves. Finance is deemed far too important to be left to the market.

Given this, regulation will need to be radically reconsidered, unless, as Mr Volker points out, we are comfortable with a substantial financial crisis every five years or so. However great the lobbying power of the financial sector, it will surely be unable to preserve a licence to commit havoc on such a scale, particularly when the new system has brought exceptional benefits to the economy generally. So far tighter regulation is desirable in the longer-run interests of the industry itself, let alone the public's. What, then, should such regulation look like? So here are seven principles of regulation. I call them the seven "Cs".

First, coverage. Perhaps the most obvious lesson is the dangers of regulatory arbitrage[①]: if the rules required certain capital requirements, institutions shifted activities into off-balance-sheet vehicles; if rules operated restrictively in one jurisdiction, activities were shifted elsewhere; and if certain institutions were more tightly regulated, then activities shifted to others. Regulatory coverage must be complete. All leveraged institutions above a certain size must be inside the net.

Second, cushions. Equity capital is the most important cushion in the financial system. Also helpful is subordinated debt. If Bear Stearns had had larger equity capital, the authorities might not have needed to rescue it.

---

① arbitrage [ˈɑːbitrɑːʒ] *n.* 套利

贝尔斯登的经验对我们的提醒，由于政府不敢放手，我们不可能拥有这种方式。 政府认为，公众必须受到银行的保护，而银行则必须明哲保身。 政府认为财政大权举足轻重，不能将其投放市场。

沃尔克先生指出，鉴于这种情况，我们需要从根本上重新考虑金融监管机制，除非我们对每 5 年左右一次的严重的金融危机置若罔闻。 不管金融部门的游说力量如何庞大，它肯定无法批准如此大规模的破坏行为，特别是新系统给实体经济带来超凡实惠之际。 到目前为止，就行业本身的长期利益而言，更严格的监管是可取的，更不用说公众的态度了。 那么，这种规则应该是什么样的呢？ 以下就是金融监管的七条原则。 我称之为七"C"规则。

第一，覆盖范围。 也许最明显的教训是监管套利的危险：如果规则有一定的资本要求，机构则需要将活动纳入资产负债表中运作；如果规则在司法程序下严格运行，活动则转向别处；如果某些机构更加严格地监管，那么这些活动就会转移到其他地方。 监管的覆盖面必须完整。 所有超过一定规模的杠杆机构都必须置于监管之下。

第二，缓冲。 权益资本是金融体系最重要的缓冲。 次级债务也有好处。 如果贝尔斯登握有较大的股本，可能不会需要当局的救助。 在整个金融体系中，资本的必要条件必须相同，以此应对任何特定类别的风险。 但也必须对其他的缓冲给予足够多的注意，如流动资金。

第三，承诺。 毫无疑问，目前的贷款并证券化模式存在着巨大的缺陷：贷款人没有充分意识到计划出售给他人的贷款的质量。 在沃伦·巴菲特看来，他们没有"在博弈中蜕变"。 即使不是不负责

Capital requirements must be the same across the entire financial system, against any given class of risks. But there must also be greater attention to the adequacy of that other cushion: liquidity.

Third, commitment. The originate-and-distribute model has, it is now clear, a huge drawback: originators do not care sufficiently about the quality of loans they plan to offload on to others. They do not, in Warren Buffett's phrase, have "skin in the game". That makes for sloppy, if not irresponsible or even fraudulent lending. Originators should be required, therefore, to hold equity portions of securitised loans.

Fourth, cyclicality. Existing rules are pro-cyclical. Capital evaporates in bad times, as a result of write-offs, thereby forcing contraction of lending, worsening the economic slowdown and further impairing assets. Mark-to-market accounting, though inherently desirable, has a similar effect. One solution could be to differentiate between target levels of capital and a lower minimum level. Institutions that have minimum capital in bad times would only be required to aim for the higher target level over an extended period.

Fifth, clarity. Lack of information, asymmetric① information and uncertainty are inherent in financial activities. These are why they are vulnerable to swings in collective mood. The transactions-orientated financial system is particularly vulnerable, because information has to flow freely across arms-length markets. So a big challenge is to generate as much clarity as is possible. One issue is the calamitous② recent role of the rating agencies and the conflicts of interest under which they operate.

Sixth, complexity. Excessive complexity is a significant source of lack

---

① asymmetric [ˌæsɪˈmetrɪk] *adj.* 不对称的
② calamitous [kəˈlæmɪtəs] *adj.* 多灾难的

任、甚至欺诈性的贷款，也是一种草率的行为。因此，应该要求贷款人持有部分证券贷款的股权。

第四，周期性。现行的规则都是顺周期性的。由于债务勾销，资本在萧条期蒸发，从而迫使贷款萎缩，加剧经济的放缓，并进一步损害资产。按市值计价也有类似的效果，但本质上合情合理。解决办法之一是区分资金的目标水平和较低的最小值水平。机构在萧条期的最低注册资本应该只为了实现扩张期的更高目标水平。

第五，透明度。缺乏信息、信息不对称和不确定性是金融活动的固有特征。这就是为什么他们很容易在集体情绪的影响下波动。由于信息在差异的市场上自由流动，交易导向型的金融系统就显得特别脆弱。因此，一个巨大的挑战就是尽可能形成透明度。近期存在的一个问题是，在评级机构的操作下，他们扮演了灾难性的角色，并引发了利益冲突。

第六，复杂性。过度的复杂性是缺乏透明度的一个重要原因。正如我们已经看到的那样，它对贷款并证券化模式贻害无穷，因为市场有时对复杂的证券产品失去控制，迫使中央银行将成为"市场庄家的最后手段"，承担所有的困难。那么，一种可能性就是坚持所有的衍生品在交易所完成交易。

第七，赔偿。在这方面，我能做的没有比引用沃尔克先生的话更好了："如果适当地统一激励机制，成功的交易和贷款发放者就可以得到丰厚的回报。当失败接踵而至之时，调整激励措施的魔咒似乎在实施对称损失的失利中消耗殆尽。"监管机构能否采取一些有效措施尚不清楚。

of clarity. It is particularly damaging, as we have seen, to the originate-and-distribute model, because markets in complex securitised products may, at times, seize up, forcing central banks to become "market makers of last resort", with all the difficulties this entails. One possibility then is to insist that all derivatives be traded on exchanges.

Seventh, compensation. On this I can do no better than quote Mr. Volcker: "In the name of properly aligning① incentives, there are enormous rewards for successful trades and for loan originators. The mantra② of aligning incentives seems to be lost in the failure to impose symmetrical losses — or frequently any loss at all — when failures ensue." Whether regulators can do anything effective is unclear.

John Maynard Keynes wrote of an eighth "c". He argued that "when the capital development of a country becomes a byproduct of the activities of a casino, the job is likely to be ill done". He had a point. Features of a casino will always be present in a financial system that performs the essential functions of guarding people's savings and allocating them where they can do most good.

Regulation will always be highly imperfect. But an effort must still be made to improve it.

(966 words)

---

① aligning [əˈlainiŋ] n. 对准
② mantra [ˈmæntrə] n. 颂歌

约翰·梅纳德·凯恩斯提出了第八个"C"。他认为，"当一个国家的资本发展成为赌场活动的副产品，这项工作就可能出现病态"。他有这样一个观点，赌场的特点将永远出现在金融体系中，它履行着基本的职能：保卫人民的储蓄，并将这些储蓄分配到它们最能发挥效用的地方。

即使监管永远呈高度不完美的状态，但我们仍然必须做出努力，完善监管系统。

知识链接 🔍

Northern Rock 北岩银行目前是英国的一家国有银行，也是主要的住房按揭银行之一。在伦敦，提起北岩银行，人们就会想到住房按揭。很少有人在北岩存款，但都知道北岩的按揭利率是全伦敦最优惠的贷款。

题　记

　　不知从何时起，美国媒体开始流行一种说法，即华尔街和主街。当然，华尔街指的是以华尔街为代表的金融机构、金融市场和金融体系；而顾名思义，主街指的是金融体系之外的传统产业、传统市场乃至普罗大众。华尔街与主街之间的巨大鸿沟正在弥合：华尔街不再是美国主体经济的附属品，主街在美国的经济生活中起着越来越重要的作用。但是，投资领域的华尔街品牌和消费领域的主街品牌正面临着同样的困境，即如何取得消费者对品牌的信任。鼻青脸肿的华尔街金融人士们纷纷要求美联储刺激经济、恢复金融市场流动性；义正词严的主街领袖则要求给一点教训，纠正过度贪婪与追逐风险的华尔街思维，否则"主街"的实体经济健康会受到影响。道琼斯工业平均指数戏剧化的波动证实，华尔街的焦虑正在成为主街的烦恼。

Wall Street's Angst
is now Main Street's

Financial-services brands must regain value and build trust not only in the business community but also with consumers amid banks' implosion.[①] Branding isn't simply a case of slapping a logo on a business. It's about understanding the revenue flows, the risks, the role of the brand, its competitive strength, and its relationship with staff and consumers across multiple business segments.

Take a careful look at the brands that have been in the headlines in the past week. Some of these brands are what we'd call "Wall Street" brands. Others could be defined loosely as "Main Street" brands. It is just as it sounds: Wall Street brands position themselves to the investment community, while Main Street brands position themselves to the consumer. Lehman Brothers is, or should I say was, a Wall Street brand. Bank of America, on the other hand, is a Main Street brand. And there are some within the financial-services sector that are both Wall Street and Main Street — such as Merrill Lynch — which for business, service or

---

① implosion [im'pləuʒən] n. 破裂

华尔街的焦虑成为主街的烦恼

金融服务品牌必须重获价值，不仅要在商界，而且要在动荡的银行内部与消费者建立一种相互信任的关系。创建品牌并不是简单地给企业贴标签。它是收益流通、风险、品牌角色、竞争力强度以及多个企业部门之间员工与消费者的融会贯通。

细心观察一下过去一周新闻提要中的品牌名称。有一些被我们称为"华尔街品牌"，还有一些被广义地定为"主街品牌"。正如通常所说：华尔街品牌把自己定位在投资领域，而主街品牌把自己定位在消费领域。或如我所知，雷曼兄弟属于华尔街品牌；而从另一个角度来看，美国的银行归属于主街品牌。还有一些金融服务部门内部的品牌，如美林证券公司，既具有华尔街的品牌价值，也带有主街品牌的特征。由于商业、服务或声誉等种种原因，这些公司管理交叉领域的综合业务。

没有人在陷入僵局时还真正关心华尔街品牌，更谈不上关注华尔街。想一想贝尔斯登、潘恩韦伯和添惠。这些公司已经倒闭，尽管华尔街与金融界直接相关，也许甚至与工商业界利害攸关，但主街上没有人对此过分在意。你的主街日常金融服务客户刚刚茅塞顿开、意识到问题严重程度的时候，这些问题已经在金融界蔓延了

reputation reasons, manage to cross boundaries into the general consciousness.

When the going gets tough, no one really cares about Wall Street brands — not even Wall Street. Think of Bear Stearns, Paine Webber and Dean Witter. All have died, and while it concerned the immediate financial community and maybe even the business community, no one on Main Street cared that much. Meanwhile, on Main Street, your everyday financial-services consumer is just beginning to understand the extent of the troubles that have been developing in the sector in the past year. Consumers are asking tough questions, confidence is in decline and the two streets are merging in order to avoid further failure. Wall Street's angst is now Main Street's angst, as evident in the dramatic swings of the Dow Jones Industrial Average. Investor confidence is at an all-time low, and the news and economic analyses, not to mention respected figures such as George Soros, only seem to perpetuate① fears, forecasting that the worst is yet to come. It is now obvious to everyone on Main Street that financial brands are in trouble — and may have been in trouble for some time now.

So what is it that's fundamentally wrong with financial-services brands? Why are brands such as Lehman Brothers and AIG caving so disastrously, rather than being immune to these crises? Certainly one of the factors that has accelerated the problem relates to the common use of a "masterbrand" strategy: From Bank of America to Merrill Lynch to Citigroup to AIG, we can see all of a brand's business units tied together

---

① perpetuate [pə'petʃueit] vt. 使人记住不忘

整整一年。 消费者们提出了一些尖锐的问题,他们的信心在下降,为了避免进一步的破产,两街正在合并。 道琼斯工业平均指数戏剧化的波动证实,华尔街的焦虑正在成为主街的烦恼。 投资者的信心空前低落,新闻和经济分析看起来只能继续增加人们的担忧,他们预测最糟糕的情况尚未到来,更不用说受人推崇的乔治·索罗斯指数。 主街上的每个人现在心知肚明,金融品牌已经陷入困境,这种困境到目前为止可能已经持续了一段时间。

那么,金融服务品牌最根本的错误是什么呢? 为什么雷曼兄弟和美国国际集团等品牌会落得如此悲惨的境地,对危机如此缺乏免疫力呢? 加剧问题的因素之一显然与频繁使用"主品牌"战略相关。 我们可以看到,从美国银行到美林、花旗和美国国际集团,品牌的业务单位全都与单一的公司品牌资产捆绑。 这种方式是一把双刃剑。 虽然在繁荣时期每个人似乎都能获利,但是在萧条时期,所有的负面效应都会影响整个董事会。 如果你随我而动,投资银行的困难时期也会拉响消费者的警报。 创建品牌并不是简单地给企业贴标签,它是收益流通、风险、品牌角色、竞争力强度以及多个企业部门之间员工与消费者的融会贯通。 简而言之,它是对无形资本的理解,对最大限度地创造企业价值起着杠杆的作用。

如果我是金融服务行业的首席营销官,我就会让我自己和我的团队考虑这些重大的问题。 我们在世界范围内观察我们的品牌价值,这些证据表明,华尔街和主街在提升品牌的杠杆作用、影响消费者决策方面仍然存在着很大的空间。 对美国银行和美林证券来说,这是华尔街和主街合并的起点,但是美国银行现在面临的最大问题是在何处接管美林证券的业务和品牌。 为了制定这个决策,他

under one asset, the corporate brand. This approach can be a double-edged sword. While in the good times everyone appears to benefit, in bad times any negative impacts will be felt across the board. A bad day in investment banking can alarm the consumer, if you follow my drift. Branding isn't simply a case of slapping a logo on a business. It's about understanding the revenue flows, the risks, the role of the brand, its competitive strength, and its relationship with staff and consumers across multiple business segments. In short, it's understanding the intangible asset and leveraging it to best create value for the business.

If I were a financial-services CMO, these are the big questions I would be asking myself and my team. The evidence we've seen from our brand valuations around the globe certainly suggest there is plenty of room for improvement in leveraging the role of the brand in consumers' decision-making, both on Wall Street and on Main Street. While this has to be the starting point when Wall Street and Main Street merge, as with Bank of America and Merrill Lynch, the big question facing Bank of America right now must be where to take the Merrill Lynch business and brand. In order to make that decision, they must first understand the role of the Merrill Lynch brand and its ultimate brand value.

Brands drive decisions and demand, and clarity on these points must be the starting point for any new strategy for Merrill Lynch within the Bank of America portfolio. Once that's understood, we can view the brand in isolation from the business, remove the parts of Merrill Lynch that are clearly broken and begin to rebuild. There's still value there — at least $ 50 billion worth, and $ 11.4 billion of that was brand value at

们必须首先理解美林品牌的角色和它最终的品牌价值。

品牌推动了决策和需求，要弄清楚这些观点必须以美林证券在美国银行的投资组合新战略为起点。 一旦明白了这一点，我们可以查看该品牌在企业中的隔离业务，剥离美林证券已经破产的部分，并开始重建。 美林证券的价值仍然存在，至少值 500 亿美元，其中114 亿美元的品牌价值是由国际品牌集团计算出来的，出现在国际品牌集团创建的全球最有价值的品牌排名之中。 虽然人们认为保持这个数字有点乐观，但我们必须记住，美林在未来仍然拥有相当大的价值。 美国国际集团与美林不同，他是华尔街的一个大品牌，拥有美国国际集团的汽车和其他企业建立起来的庞大消费群体和主街的极度信任。 美国国际集团必须十分小心谨慎，要避免丧失消费者的信任度。 在这种情况下，尽管华尔街处于混乱的关键期，活跃的主街仍可以相安无事。 表面看来，主街不太一样，但充满挑战的经济对品牌的保值和增值提供了机会。 在困难时期，消费者们越来越依赖品牌，从而为自己制定购买决策。 另一个判断因素是品牌优势，它取决于品牌经营者如何对新的市场环境做出反应。

最后，首席执行官和首席营销官的最大问题是接下来做什么？首先，永远不要惊慌失措。 建立品牌需要很长的时间，但品牌也会在短期内土崩瓦解。 在我们看到的晚间新闻中，首席执行官和首席营销官很容易觉察品牌的需要，并立即做出某些改变，也许是出于无奈，甚或只是试图向世界证明你做了一些事。 不管动机是什么，这肯定是一个错误的策略。 记住：品牌和品牌价值要靠时间来建立。 虽然战略需要一致，但战术需要根据短期形势进行调整。

the time Interbrand created the Best Global Brands ranking. Although one may argue that maintaining that figure is a little optimistic, we must remember that Merrill Lynch still has considerable future value. AIG, not unlike Merrill Lynch, is a huge Wall Street brand but has strong consumer presence and tremendous Main Street trust established by businesses such as AIG Auto and others. AIG needs to be extremely careful not to lose the trust of its consumers. In this case, actively reassuring Main Street despite the Wall Street turmoil is critical. Although it may not seem like it on the surface, a challenging economy is an opportunity for brands to create and secure value. In difficult times, customers increasingly rely on brands for their decision making. The second part of the equation is brand strength, which will depend on how brand managers respond to the new market conditions.

Finally, the big question for CEOs and CMOs will be what to do next. First of all, never panic. Brands are built over the long term but can quickly collapse in the short term. What we're watching unfold on the nightly news could easily cause CEOs and CMOs to feel that something about the brand needs to change immediately — perhaps because of a sense of helplessness or even just as an attempt to show the world you're doing something. Regardless of motive, it is certain to be a bad move. Remember: Brands and brand value take time to build. The strategy needs to stay consistent, but the tactics need to address the short-term issues.

(993 words)

华尔街的焦虑成为主街的烦恼

Wall Street 华尔街是纽约市曼哈顿区南部从百老汇路延伸到东河的一条街道的名字，从百老汇到东河仅有 7 个街段。华尔街全长不过三分之一英里，宽仅 11 米，是英文"墙街"的音译。它的前身是 1792 年荷兰殖民者为抵御英军侵犯而建筑的一堵土墙，从东河一直筑到哈德逊河，后沿墙形成的一条街，因而得名华尔街。然而，华尔街却以"美国的金融中心"闻名于世。美国摩根财阀、洛克菲勒石油大王和杜邦财团等开设的银行、保险、航运、铁路等公司的经理处，以及著名的纽约证券交易所全都集中在这条街。

Main street 主街。在北美媒体中，"主街"通常代表日常工人和小企业主的利益，有时候和象征着企业资本主义的"华尔街"相对。不知从何时起，美国媒体开始流行一种说法，即华尔街和主街。当然，华尔街指的是以华尔街为代表的金融机构、金融市场和金融体系；而顾名思义，主街指的是金融体系之外的传统产业、传统市场乃至普罗大众。

题　记

　　资本主义体系在金融危机的冲击下似乎溃不成军，资本主义制度的拥趸们如热锅上的蚂蚁，急不可耐地出谋划策。任期所剩不到三个月的美国总统布什召集时任法国总统萨科奇和欧盟主席巴罗佐在日理万机之际会晤于华盛顿，商讨尽快举行各国领导人峰会，以期稳定世界金融体系，建立新的金融秩序。布什宣布抵制经济孤立主义政策的危险诱惑，继续执行提高公民的生活水准。萨科奇提出了评级机构改革和探索未来货币制度的想法。前任英国首相戈登·布朗也主张对全球资本主义制度进行根本性的变革，包括建立跨境机制来监测全球最大的金融机构。金融危机动摇了世界对西方资本主义制度的信心，促使西方社会不得不直面如何实现资本主义自身的救赎。

Fixing the World
Financial System

President Bush, looking for answers to a global economic emergency with just three months left in office, will host an international summit to discuss ways to fix the world financial system but warned on Saturday against reforms that threaten capitalism. "We will work to strengthen and modernize our nations' financial systems so we can help ensure that this crisis doesn't happen again, " Bush said at the Camp David presidential retreat.

Bush, meeting with French President Nicolas Sarkozy and European Commission President Jose Manuel Barroso, did not announce a date or site for the summit. But Sarkozy suggested it be held in the shadow of Wall Street before the end of November. "Insofar as the crisis began in New York, then the global solution must be found to this crisis in New York, " Sarkozy said.

In a joint statement issued after their slightly more than 2 1/2-hour visit, the three leaders said they would contact other nations next week about having a summit in the United States soon after the presidential

修复世界金融体系

　　任期所剩不到三个月的美国总统布什，为寻求应对全球经济危机的解决方案，将举办一次国际峰会，讨论如何修复世界金融体系，但他在本周六又警告说，改革会威胁到资本主义体系。 布什在戴维营总统度假胜地宣称："我们将努力巩固国家的金融体系，并使之现代化，以确保不再爆发金融危机。"

　　布什在会见法国总统尼古拉·萨科齐和欧盟执委会主席巴罗佐时并没有公布首脑会议的日期或地点。 但是，萨科齐建议，11月底之前将在华尔街的阴影下举行这场活动。 萨科齐认为，"既然这次危机首先从纽约开始，那么也必须在纽约寻找解决危机的全球性方案"。

　　在超过约2个半小时的访问之后，他们发表了一份联合声明，三位领导人表示，他们下周将与其他国家商讨，美国总统选举之后是否立即在美国举行一次首脑峰会，并在随后举行一系列的首脑会议，这一切旨在解决全球经济所面临的挑战。

　　第一次首脑会议将集中讨论解决目前危机的进展，寻求意见一致，制定改革所需要的原则，以避免问题的复现和保证全球未来的繁荣。 他们认为，之后的峰会将旨在贯彻协议，采取具体步骤满足

election, then a series of subsequent summits to address the challenges facing the global economy.

The first summit would focus on progress being made to address the current crisis and seek agreement on principles of reform needed to avoid a repetition of the problems and assure global prosperity in the future. Later summits, they said, would be designed to implement agreement on specific steps to be taken to meet those principles.

Bush has backed the steps European nations have taken to fix the financial markets and is willing to listen to a range of ideas from both developed and developing nations, but he hasn't signed on to the more ambitious, broad-stroke reforms that some European leaders have in mind to avoid a repeat of the market crisis that rippled around the globe.

Sarkozy has floated the idea of reforming rating agencies and even exploring the future of currency systems. British Prime Minister Gordon Brown, who engineered a British bank bailout that inspired U.S. and European rescues, is proposing radical changes to the global capitalist system, including a cross-border mechanism to monitor the world's 30 biggest financial institutions.

Standing outside on a crisp autumn day at the helipad on the secluded retreat, all three leaders spoke soberly about what Bush called a "trying time for all our nations." "As we make the regulatory and institutional changes necessary to avoid a repeat of this crisis, it is essential that we preserve the foundations of democratic capitalism — a commitment to free markets, free enterprise, and free trade," Bush

这些原则。

布什表示，他将大力支持欧洲国家为修复金融市场而采取的步骤，并愿意听取发达国家和发展中国家的各种意见。有些欧洲领导人为避免波及全球的市场危机重现，打算雄心勃勃、大刀阔斧地制定改革计划，但布什对此举并不赞同。

萨科齐已经提出了评级机构改革和探索未来货币制度的想法。英国首相戈登·布朗救助英国银行业的工程鼓舞了美国和欧洲的救援工作，他主张对全球资本主义制度进行根本性的变革，包括建立一个跨境机制来监测全球 30 家最大金融机构。

在一个秋高气爽的日子，三位领导人站在外面僻静的停机坪上，严肃地谈论着布什所谓的"考验我们所有国家的时刻"。布什说："为避免危机再度发生，我们必须制定监管和体制方面的变革方案。我们必须维护民主资本主义的基础，即恪守自由市场、自由企业和自由贸易的体制。我们必须抵制经济孤立主义的危险诱惑，继续实行开放市场的政策，提高生活水准，帮助全球数以百万计的人摆脱贫困。"

2007 年的一天，道琼斯指数突破 14 000 点之际，投资者在养老基金、大学储蓄计划、401k 计划和其他投资上已经失去了 8.3 万亿美元。国会通过了布什政府 7 000 亿美元的救市计划，收购银行及其他机构的不良资产，以支撑金融业。危机震撼了世界各地的金融市场，引起全球性的经济衰退恐慌。布什呼吁人们耐心地等待救市措施生效："我们正在处理一个重要的问题。但美国人民和我们世界各地的朋友应该知道，我们有信心让这些措施起作用。"

巴罗佐认为，是改革整个国际金融体系的时候了。他声称：

said. "We must resist the dangerous temptation of economic isolationism and continue the policies of open markets that have lifted standards of living and helped millions of people escape poverty around the world."

Since one day in 2007, when the Dow topped 14,000, investors have lost $ 8.3 trillion from pension funds, college savings plans, 401 (k) s and other investments. Congress gave Bush a $ 700 billion plan to buy bad assets from banks and other institutions to shore up the financial industry. The crisis has rocked financial markets across the world, prompting fears of a worldwide recession. "We're dealing with a significant problem," Bush said, calling for patience to let rescue measures take effect. "But the American people and our friends around the world can know that we have confidence that the measures will work."

Barroso said it was time for the entire international financial system to be reformed. "We need a new global financial order," he said. "The European Union and the U.S., we can make a difference together."

Sarkozy also stressed the urgency of what he said was a "worldwide crisis" that demands a "worldwide solution." He said he agreed with Bush's view that reforms challenge the foundations of market economics. But he added: "We cannot continue along the same lines because the same problems will trigger the same disasters." He said hedge funds and tax havens① cannot continue to operate as they have in the past; financial

---

① haven ['heivn] *n.* 安全地方

"我们需要一个新的全球金融秩序。 欧盟和美国可以联手有所作为。"

萨科齐也强调了这种观点，他认为"全球危机"迫切需要一个"全球解决方案"。 他说，他同意布什的观点，改革会挑战市场经济的基础。 但他补充道："我们不能继续沿着原有的路线前进，因为同样的问题会引发同样的灾难。"他指出，对冲基金和避税场所不能再继续承袭往常的运作手段，必须对金融机构实施监控。 萨科齐说："不再可能接受这种状况。 我们需要改变。 这种资本主义是对我们所信仰的资本主义的背叛。"

白宫副发言人托尼·法拉托在电话中对记者说，布什总统希望确保改革，放宽贸易限制，减缓贸易自由化或阻碍资本在国家间的流动。 但他认为，"我们确实需要找到增加透明度的办法，特别是确保主要经济体有能力抵御系统内部的事件，如我们正在处理的事件"。

法拉托说，各国领导人提出多举行几次峰会，因为金融危机中的问题涉及面很宽，关系到很多国家的生死存亡。 他指出，有理由推测，第一次峰会将在11月大选日后举行，但时机很大程度上取决于众多国家的领导人能够在很短的一段时间内相聚。 他说，峰会不一定非得在纽约举行。 当选总统的观点，无论是约翰·麦凯恩还是巴拉克·奥巴马，将在讨论中扮演重要的角色，但他认为，当选总统是否出席第一次峰会还是个未知数。

institutions cannot continue without supervisory control. "This is no longer acceptable," Sarkozy said. "This is no longer possible. This sort of capitalism is a betrayal of the sort of capitalism we believe in."

White House deputy press secretary Tony Fratto said in a telephone call with reporters that the president wants to make sure that reforms do not restrict trade, slow down trade liberalization or impede the flow of capital between nations. But he said: "We do need to find ways to increase transparency① and ensure that major economies, in particular, have the ability to prevent systematic events like what we're dealing with now."

Fratto said the leaders proposed more than one summit because of the breadth of issues in the financial meltdown and the number of countries involved. He said it was reasonable to assume that the first summit would be in November, after Election Day, but the timing was largely dependent on being able to get leaders from many nations together in a short period of time. He said it would not necessarily be in New York. The views of the president-elect, be it John McCain or Barack Obama, would be important in the discussion, but he said he could not say whether the president-elect would attend the first summit.

(891 words)

① transparency [træns'pɛərənsi] *n.* 透明度

知识链接

The Camp David 戴维营。戴维营位于马里兰州的卡托克廷山地国家公园，是美国总统的度假胜地。戴维营始建于 1938 年，最初名为"卡托克廷山庄"，是卡托克廷山地三大公共游乐园之一，位于首都华盛顿西北 120 公里处的马里兰州卡托克廷山间，海拔约 548.6 米，占地约 5 平方公里，乘直升机由白宫出发到此只需要短短的 30 分钟。整个度假营地由若干个乡村别墅组成，有 10 多幢石木结构的乡村式平房。主要建筑是四幢称为山杨屋、桦木屋、月季屋和山茱萸屋的木屋，其中山杨屋是总统的寓所。从山上远眺，周围环绕的国家公园一览无余、尽收眼底，令人心旷神怡。

题　记

　　自由经济市场在繁荣美国经济的同时也埋下了金融危机的伏笔。为了恢复人们对美国金融体系的信心，同时促进银行贷款再次开始在消费者和企业之间正常运行，纽约联邦政府实施了一系列的关键性举措，希望救活溃败的金融体系。财政部计划在各类银行购买高级优先股，以帮助银行继续给企业和个人提供贷款。美国联邦存款保险公司将会"暂时性地保证"被保险银行的大部分最新负债，并扩大对所有未被列入救市计划银行的政府保险，同时对小企业通常使用的不含息银行账户提供存款保险，保证他们的运营。美联储启动了大萧条时代的机制购买大量的短期债务，以此打破信用萎缩的局面。但这些显然不是来自外部的首次金融救助活动。

Rescue Plan

The federal government announced a historic plan to restore confidence in the U.S. financial system and to spur banks to begin lending again more normally — both to each other and to consumers and businesses. Here are the key elements that will be put in place first:

1. Buying equity in banks

The Treasury will buy up to $ 250 billion in senior preferred shares in a wide variety of banks. Nine of the largest banks have agreed to be the first institutions in which the government takes a stake. But the program will be available potentially to thousands of banks. The government may take senior preferred shares up to the lesser of $ 25 billion or 3% of the bank's risk-weighted assets. The stakes will come largely in the form of non-voting shares and may be sold to a third-party if the government wishes. The shares will pay 5% a year in dividends for the first five years and 9% after that. The increase in the dividend may serve as incentive for the banks — if they have the private capital to do it — to buy back the government's shares before the five years are up. The government will also receive warrants[①] to buy additional shares worth up to 15% of the preferred stock it buys. The strike price for Uncle Sam: the average price the stock was selling for over

----

① warrant ['wɔrənt] *n.* 许可证

救 市 举 措

联邦政府宣布了一项历史性的方案，旨在重建对美国金融业的信心，刺激银行之间、银行与消费者、企业之间贷款的再次正常运转。 以下是该方案需要优先实施的关键性举措：

1. 购买银行股本

财政部计划将在各类银行购买多达2 500亿美元的高级优先股。九家最大的银行已经同意成为第一批将股份转让给政府的机构。 但是，该方案可能会适用于成千上万有潜在能力的银行。 政府可能收购低于 250 亿美元或占银行风险加权资产 3% 的高级优先股。 风险主要来自非投票权的股份，如果政府愿意的话，可以将其出售给第三方。 政府购买的优先股头 5 年将获得 5% 的年股息，其后增至9% 。 如果银行认筹私人资本来完成这项交易，增加的红利可以刺激银行在 5 年内回购政府的股票。 政府还有权增持最多相当于其注资 15% 的普通股。 山姆大叔敲定的价格是：在 20 天的时间内，股票卖出的平均价格超出政府购买优先股的价格。

斯坦福集团的金融服务分析师嘉略特·赛博格认为，鉴于银行股份在过去一周连受重创，如果政府能很快地行使其股票认证权，就有可能从其对排名前九的银行的投资项目中获利。 斯坦福集团是

the 20-day period preceding the government's purchase of preferred shares.

Given the battering bank shares have taken in the past week, if the government exercises its warrants soon, it is likely to make a profit from its investment in the first nine banks in the program, said Jaret Seiberg, financial services analyst at The Stanford Group, a policy research firm. Participants in the program will be subject to the restrictions on executive compensation that Congress included in the financial rescue law that it passed. One such measure, for example, requires that any bonus or incentive paid to a senior executive officer for targets met will have to be repaid if it's later proven that earnings or profit statements were inaccurate.

2. Backing new debt from banks

The Federal Deposit Insurance Corp. will guarantee new, senior unsecured debt issued by banks, thrifts and bank holding companies. The new debt that will be covered must mature within three years, and banks may opt in to this program. The intent is to give confidence to the buyers of bank debt that they will get paid back no matter what. The program will be paid for by user fees imposed on banks. No taxpayer dollars or dollars from the FDIC insurance fund will be used.

3. Providing more coverage for bank deposits

The FDIC will temporarily provide unlimited coverage for all non-interest-bearing accounts, which typically are those where businesses park money to cover their near-term expenses such as payroll. The increased coverage will last through the end of the year. The program will be paid for by user fees that are part of the premium the bank pays the FDIC to insure deposits. No taxpayer dollars or dollars from the FDIC insurance fund will be used. The goal is to boost liquidity for otherwise healthy banks — particularly regional and local ones — that might otherwise have

一家政策研究公司。 该方案的参与者将接受高管薪酬制约，国会通过的金融救助法案包含薪酬制约条款。 例如，有一项此类措施要求，如果后期证明收入或利润报表有误，达成目标的高级管理人员必须偿还之前获得的奖金或奖励。

2. 支持银行的新债务

美国联邦存款保险公司计划为银行、储蓄机构和银行控股公司发行的新型、高级无担保债务提供担保。 新债务 3 年内到期，银行可以选择加入这一计划。 这么做的目的是让银行债权人有信心，无论如何他们都会获得回报。 该方案将由强加给银行的用户费用来支付，不会使用纳税人的钱或联邦存款保险公司的保险基金。

3. 为银行存款提供更多的覆盖率

联邦存款保险公司将为所有无息账户暂时提供无限期覆盖，这通常是商业机构用来弥补工资等短期开支的资金。 增加的覆盖率将持续到今年年底。 该计划将由用户支付费用，这些费用是银行支付联邦存款保险公司投保存款的部分保险费，不会动用纳税人的钱或联邦存款保险公司的保险基金。 此项计划的目标是为其他健康运营的银行增加流动资金，尤其是区域银行和地方银行，否则紧张的储户会撤出他们的资金，转投较大的金融机构。

4. 购买短期商业票据

美联储正在敲定一项临时计划，打算购买商业票据市场的各家公司签发的为期 3 个月的高品质债券。 最近大幅度削减的商业票据市场是过去用于支付许多国家大公司和金融机构业务费用的主要资金来源。 这项计划的目的在于保证有人购买债务，从而让私人买家更有信心，如果他们也购买公司的短期债券，资金会迅速回笼。 这

seen nervous depositors pull their money out in favor of putting them at larger institutions.

4. Buy short-term commercial paper

The Federal Reserve is finalizing plans for a temporary program in which it will buy high-quality three-month debt issued by businesses in the commercial paper market. The commercial paper market, which has been sharply curtailed recently, is the prime source of funding used to cover operating costs at many of the nation's largest companies and financial institutions. The intent of the program is to guarantee there will be a buyer of the debt, which in turn will make private-sector buyers more confident that they will get paid back if they, too, buy a company's short-term debt. That's because the company pays back debt holders by issuing new commercial paper.

But what about buying troubled assets? When the government's rescue plan was first formally proposed little more than two weeks ago, the major initiative was supposed to be the purchase of troubled assets off of banks' balance sheets. The rationale: Banks are having a hard time attracting capital because there is concern that they may be holding so-called "toxic" assets. Those assets have underlying value but no one has known how to price them in the wake of the housing crisis.

The four major steps the government announced do not preclude the Treasury from pursuing its asset-purchase option. Indeed, Treasury and White House officials have indicated they are still working on structuring a program to buy troubled assets, which the government could hold until the market recovers and then sell back to investors at a profit. But it clearly isn't going to be the first effort out of the gate.

(859 words)

是因为公司通过发行新的商业票据来偿付债权人。

但是怎样收购问题资产呢？ 两个多星期前，政府首次正式提出救市计划，主要的倡议被认为是购买银行资产负债表中的不良资产。 其理念是：由于人们担心他们可能会购买到所谓的"有毒"资产，所以银行难以吸引投资。 这些资产虽然有潜在的价值，但是在随之而来的住房危机冲击下，没有人知道如何对它们估价。

政府宣布了以上四个主要步骤，但并不排除财政部购买其资产的可能。 事实上，财政部和白宫的官员们指出，他们仍在致力于构建收购不良资产的方案，政府在市场恢复前将掌控这些不良资产，之后会卖给投资者获取一定的利润。 但这些显然不是来自外部的首次金融救助活动。

知识链接

Federal Deposit Insurance Corporation（*FDIC*） 美国联邦储蓄保险公司。美国联邦储蓄保险公司于 1933 年创立，旨在维护公众信心和金融系统的稳定，为美国的储户提供存款保险机制。如果会员银行发生破产或无法偿还债务的危机时，美国联邦储蓄保险公司将为这个会员银行的每个储户提供最高限额为 10 万美元的存款保险。

题　记

　　经济全球化的背景下，越来越多的谈判超越国家边界在跨文化环境中发生。文化差异对跨国谈判而言，成为极其重要而又繁琐的变量。当双方跨越文化进行谈判的时候，各自的文化明目张胆地摆到了谈判桌上。如果美国推销员向沙特阿拉伯的潜在客户推销价值数百万美元的猪皮黏合剂，无疑会被穆斯林文化定位为邪恶的行为。而德国的工人与监事会的监事几乎拥有同等的代表权，则会让北美体验过基于集体管理的股票持有人的管理人员惊诧不已。当意大利的轮胎制造商"倍耐力"企图收购其德国的竞争对手"欧洲橡胶"时，文化差异的潜藏挑战使"倍耐力"损失惨重。所以，文化经常以一种微妙的方式影响人们的谈判态度与谈判行为。这种效应好似"以石投水"，石子激起涟漪，向整个池面漾去，文化就弥漫在整个水面之中，并且渗透在谈判的方方面面。

The Hidden Challenge
of Cross-Border Negotiations

Cultural differences can influence business negotiations in unexpected ways, as many a hapless① deal maker has learned. But the differences extend well beyond surface behaviors, such as proper table manners and the exchange of business cards — and even beyond deeper cultural characteristics, such as attitudes about relationships and deadlines. Indeed, there's another, equally treacherous aspect to cross-border negotiation: the ways that people from different regions come to agreement or the processes involved in negotiations. Decision-making and governance processes can vary widely from culture to culture, not only in terms of legal technicalities but also in terms of the behaviors and core beliefs that drive them. Numerous promising deals have failed because people ignored or underestimated the powerful differences in process across cultures.

① hapless [ˈhæplis] *adj.* 倒霉的

跨界谈判中隐藏的挑战

　　文化差异可以出人意料地影响商业谈判，这是许多倒霉的交易撮合人熟谙的教训。 但得体的餐桌礼仪和商业名片交换等影响远远超过了表面行为，甚至超出了对待相互关系和最后期限的态度等更深层次的文化特征。 事实上，跨界谈判还有同样变幻莫测的另外一面，即来自不同地区的人达成协议或参与谈判过程的方式。 决策制定和管理过程因文化不同而大相径庭，这种差异不仅体现在法律技术层面，也体现在驱动他们的行为和核心信念方面。 无数有望成功的交易以失败告终，就是因为人们忽略或者低估了跨文化过程中的巨大差异。

　　在某些情况下，问题在于无知或公然蔑视，正如一个美国推销员向沙特阿拉伯的潜在客户推销价值数百万美元的猪皮黏合剂，这在许多穆斯林文化中被认为是邪恶的行为。 沙特阿拉伯人毫不客气地拒绝了他的推销，并把他的公司列入沙特业务的黑名单。 但是从影响人们互动的根深蒂固的文化倾向来看，这些差异可以更为微妙，包括人们如何看待个体的作用，以及群体对待他们的态度，也就是说，包括时间或关系的重要性等一切事务。

In some cases, it's a matter of ignorance or blatant① disrespect, as with the American salesman who presented a potential Saudi Arabian client with a multimillion-dollar proposal in a pigskin binder, considered vile in many Muslim cultures. He was unceremoniously tossed out and his company blacklisted from working with Saudi businesses. But the differences can be much more subtle, arising from deep-seated cultural tendencies that influence how people interact — everything from how people view the role of the individual versus the group to their attitudes, say, about the importance of time or relationships.

In any negotiation, you are always interacting with individuals, but your real purpose is to influence a larger organization — representing a diverse set of interests — to produce a meaningful yes. In an international deal, just as at home, you need to know exactly who's involved in that larger decision process and what roles they play. But in unfamiliar territory, the answers might surprise you. Indeed, applying "home" views of corporate governance and decision making to international deals may seriously hinder the negotiation process. I find it's useful to break down the decision-making process into several constituent parts: Who are the players? Who decides what? What are the informal influences that can make or break a deal? Let's look at each of these factors, which can vary dramatically when you cross national borders.

If you're accustomed to deal making in the United States, you know

---

① blatant ['bleitnt] *adj.* 炫耀的

在任何一场谈判中，你总会和其他个体打交道，但你的真实意图是影响代表各种各样利益的更大的组织，以达到有意义的赞同。国际交易和国内交易一样，你需要确切了解谁参与到更大的决策过程，以及他们扮演什么角色。 但是在不熟悉的地域环境中，问题的答案可能会让你大吃一惊。 事实上，将"国内"集体管理和决策制定的观点运用到国际交易上可能会严重阻碍谈判进程。 我发现将决策制定过程划分为几个组成部分很有用：谁是参与者？ 谁决定什么？ 哪些非正式的影响会决定交易的成败？ 让我们来观察这些因素，每一个在跨界谈判中都可能相差悬殊。

如果你已经习惯了美国式的交易制定原则，你就会明白除去代表这两个公司之外的其他参与者都可能影响交易，他们是美国证券交易委员会、联邦贸易委员会和美国司法部。 丹尼尔·J.卡德拉克在他的著作《宇宙的主人》中写道，当旅行者集团和花旗集团考虑合并时，这两家公司的高管一起拜访了美联储主席阿兰·格林斯潘，以了解美联储的真实态度。

在国外你同样也会发现其他的参与者，但他们会不一样，并且通常都不是那么显而易见。 对那些在北美体验过基于集体管理的股票持有人的管理人员来说，发现德国的工人与监事会的监事几乎拥有同等的代表权，会让他们惊诧不已！ 在欧盟，各种布鲁塞尔委员会可能参与商业谈判。 如果收购目标有国外的子公司，那么和谈判伙伴的关系可能会更为错综复杂。 所有的赞助商都把各自的利益以及阻碍抑或促成谈判的百般解数摆上台面。 即便是其中最有经验的

that extra players beyond those representing the two companies may influence the deal: the SEC, the Federal Trade Commission, and the Justice Department, among others. In his book *Masters of the Universe*, Daniel J. Kadlec writes that when Travelers and Citicorp were contemplating a merger, the heads of both companies together visited Federal Reserve Chairman Alan Greenspan to get a reading on the Fed's likely attitude.

Abroad, you'll of course find extra players as well, but they will be different and often less obvious. For those executives experienced in North American shareholder-based corporate governance, it may come as a surprise to discover that in Germany, labor has virtually equal representation on many supervisory boards of directors. In the European Union, various Brussels commissions may get involved in business negotiations. If an acquisition target has foreign subsidiaries, the skein① of negotiating partners may grow even more tangled. All these constituencies bring their own interests to the table, as well as varying abilities to block or foster negotiations. Even GE, one of the most experienced acquirers, suffered a humiliating defeat in its attempted merger with Honeywell, in part because GE's management underestimated the nature and seriousness of European concerns about competitiveness and the potential for these concerns — and GE's European competitors — to obstruct the deal.

Another example is drawn from the research of my colleagues

---

① skein [skein] *n.* 纠纷

收购商通用电气公司，也在试图收购霍尼韦尔时惨遭失败，部分原因是通用电气公司的管理层低估了欧洲公司的本质和问题的严重性，低估了通用电气公司的竞争对手的竞争力和潜力，从而使这项交易中途夭折。

另外一个例子来自我的同事威廉·A.萨尔曼和贝尔顿·C.霍尔洛克的研究。 前苏联即将解体的时候，总部设在加州的席拉创投公司正在和俄罗斯蛋白质研究所的所长谈判，希望获得一项明显具有革命性特征的生物科技过程的所有权。 公司与该研究院的管理团队进行了马拉松式的谈判，勇敢地修复了东西方之间、商业和科学之间、官僚主义和风险资本之间的巨大差距，谈判似乎最终将导向一个双方都可以接受的协议。 虽然交易最终成功，但直到接近终点时情况才突然变得明朗，尽管莫斯科的几个部委各自坚持自己的观点和议程，也不得不批准这项协议。 如果席拉团队在早期只是墨守成规地了解真正的决策过程，就会构成人们一直预期的、潜在的致命障碍。

即便你知道有哪些人参与，如果不了解每个参与者的角色，以及谁拥有哪些决策权，那么谈判代价也会非常高昂。 例如，当意大利的轮胎制造商"倍耐力"企图收购其德国的竞争对手"欧洲橡胶"时，"倍耐力"声称它控制了欧洲橡胶的大部分股票，得到了德意志银行的默契资助，总理格哈德·施罗德的支持，以及欧洲橡胶所在地下萨克森州总理的赞同。 美国的交易仅需拥有足够股权就能使收购方控制目标，而不是这套系统。

William A. Sahlman and Burton C. Hurlock: Near the time of the collapse of the Soviet Union, California-based venture capital firm Sierra Ventures was negotiating with the director of the Institute for Protein Research in Russia, hoping to get the rights to an apparently revolutionary biotechnology process. Marathon negotiations with the institute's management team — heroically bridging huge gaps between East and West, business and science, bureaucracy and venture capital — seemed as if they would finally culminate in an acceptable deal for both sides. Although the deal ultimately succeeded, nearing the finish line it suddenly became clear that several Moscow ministries, each with its own point of view and agenda, also had to approve the agreement. This posed a potentially fatal set of obstacles that could have been anticipated had the Sierra team made more than a perfunctory① effort early on to learn about the real decision process.

Even if you know who's playing, a failure to understand each player's role — and who owns which decisions — can be very costly. For example, when Italian tire maker Pirelli sought to acquire its German rival, Continental Gummiwerke, Pirelli claimed control of a majority of Continental's shares and received tacit backing from Deutsche Bank and support from Gerhard Schröder, then Prime Minister of Lower Saxony, where Continental is based. In a U.S. transaction, merely owning enough equity often allows the acquirer to control the target. But not in this

---

① perfunctory [pə'fʌŋktəri] *adj.* 循例的

对"倍耐力"来说非常不幸的是，德国公司的管理方法提供了一个构架，可让其他重要参与者都能够阻止甚至大多数股东的意愿。尽管德国大多数大型公司的管理层有日常管理的职责，但它仅是四套参与者中的一套，还有股东、监事会和工会，它们可以在任何重大决策中起到明显的作用。更重要的是，根据劳资协同经营制度，工会选举足够半数的监事会成员，而监事会成员则选举管理委员会。而无论个人持有多少股份，管理委员会都可以阻止任何单一股东投票超过 5% 的公司股份。因此，尽管"倍耐力"声称它有效地控制了欧洲橡胶的股票，并且拥有强大的盟友，但它还是未能从所有参与者、尤其是工会和主要管理人手中获得真正的收购。这场失败的收购让这家意大利公司耗费了近 5 亿美元。

知识链接

The SEC 美国证券交易委员会，全称为：Securities and Exchange Commission。美国证券交易委员会是根据《1934 年证券交易法》于当年成立的美国联邦政府专门委员会，旨在监督证券法规的实施。委员会由 5 名委员组成，主席每 5 年更换一次，由美国总统任命。为了保证交易委员会的独立性，委员会成员不得有 3 人以上来自同一政党。美国证券交易委员会的管理条例旨在加强信息的充分披露，保护市场上公众投资利益不被玩忽职守和虚假信息所损害。美国所有的证券发行无论以何种形式出现都必须在委员会注册；所有证券交易所都在委员会监管之下；所有投资公司、投资顾问、柜台交易经纪人、做市商及所有在投资领域里从事经营的机构和个人都必须接受

setting.

Unfortunately for Pirelli, German corporate governance provides a structure in which other key players can block the will of even a majority of shareholders. While the management board in most large German companies has day-to-day management responsibilities, it is only one of four sets of players — along with shareholders, a supervisory board, and labor — that can play a significant role in any major decision. What's more, under union codetermination, labor elects fully half of the members of the supervisory board, which in turn elects the management board. And the management board can prevent any single shareholder, no matter how large his or her holdings, from voting more than 5% of the total company shares. Thus, having failed to gain real buy-in from all the players, especially labor and key managers, Pirelli couldn't complete the transaction, even though it claimed effective control over Continental's shares and had powerful allies — a humiliating defeat that cost the Italian company nearly half a billion dollars.

(980 words)

委员会的监督管理。

The Federal Trade Commission　美国联邦贸易委员会。1914 年的《联邦贸易委员会法》授权建立美国联邦贸易委员会，作为负责执行各项反托拉斯法律的行政机构。其职责范围包括：搜集和编纂情报资料、对商业组织和商业活动进行调查、对不正当的商业活动发布命令，并阻止不公平竞争。

题　记

路透社 20 年来一直在为稳定核心业务和创造一个成长的平台做着不懈的努力。总裁汤姆·格洛瑟通过一系列措施，扭转了其在信息供应、财务数据终端、基金管理者和其他财务服务公司的核心业务上的市场份额遭受巨大损失的局面。然而，彭博社对传统新闻市场的冲击，从根本上颠覆了"给苦难者慰藉，让惬意者难受"的新闻原则，将路透社逼上了重新打造品牌、转变思维观念的征途。这种"文化变革"被定义为"不让路透社的美好事物毁灭的过程"，它要"让惬意者舒适"地赚钱，为那些大把花钱的商人、掮客、消息灵通人士提供一切资讯，以便他们工作时充满自信。路透社扩大了潜在的新产品范围，改进了客服和售后维护，推出了交互式的网络电视新闻频道，将总部搬出了舰队街。这些举措帮助路透社在夺回彭博社市场份额的过程中，储备了实实在在的运营优势。

Reuters Set to Burnish[①] Its Brand

In the media business, Reuters is best known as the British-based news organization that sends journalists to far-flung corners of the world to deliver first-hand reports of conflicts and catastrophe.

But Reuters' news agency operation constitutes just 10 per cent of the 154-year-old company's revenues. Its principal business is the provision of financial data — and has, historically, always been so. German-born Paul Julius Reuter started out by using pigeons to fly stock prices between Aachen and Brussels in order to fill a gap in the telegraph link.

Reuters is the world's biggest financial data company, and Tom Glocer, the company's first chief executive to be hired from outside the news business, wants to keep it that way. But Mr. Glocer faces an uphill struggle. Several years ago, Reuters came spectacularly close to collapse. Once one of the UK's flagship companies, it was hit by the economic downturn and suffered a dramatic loss of market share to Bloomberg, its privately owned US rival, in its core business of supplying information and data terminals to banks, fund managers and other financial services companies. The company's ability to respond was hampered by a

---

① burnish [ˈbəːniʃ] vt. 磨

路透社重新打造品牌

路透社作为英国最好的新闻机构在传媒行业赫赫有名，它往世界各个遥远的角落派遣记者，并发布关于冲突和灾难的第一手报道。

但是路透集团的新闻通讯收入只占这个享有 154 年悠久历史的公司总收入的 10%。它的主要业务是提供财务数据——历史上也一直如此。德国出生的保罗·朱利叶斯·路透用信鸽在亚琛和布鲁塞尔之间传递股价，用电报连接填补了这一空白。

路透社是世界最大的财务数据公司，公司聘任的首位非传媒行业的首席执行官汤姆·格洛瑟试图维持这种模式。但是格洛瑟先生正面临一场艰苦的斗争。几年前，路透社濒临倒闭，令所有人大跌眼镜。路透社是曾经的英国旗舰公司之一，但在经济低迷时期遭受重创，银行、基金管理者和其他财务服务公司的信息供应、数据终端等核心业务损失惨重，市场份额流向它的美国竞争对手、私营业主彭博社。在自我陶醉的几十年间，它本身的市场占有率形成了一个臃肿、效率低下的结构，牵制了公司应对市场的能力。

由于近期可能是顾客取消订阅的关键时间，公司正在认真考虑即将公布的一季度交易声明。随着格洛瑟先生的三年重组计划进入

bloated①, inefficient structure built up during decades of complacency when it had the market all to itself.

A first-quarter trading statement, to be released, is being keenly anticipated as the recent period can be a key month for customers to cancel subscriptions. It is being published as Mr. Glocer's three-year restructuring program — known as Fast Forward — enters its final year. The view from investors and customers is encouraging. "The heavy lifting has been done and investors are looking to Reuters with a view that the company has by and large been fixed," says Paul Richards, an analyst at Numis Securities, the stockbroker. "They feel Tom Glocer has done a very good job and they are looking at the pace of the financial services recovery and where Reuters goes from here."

The company is already ahead of its targets to cut costs by £440m and to cut 3,000 jobs from a base of 16,000 — which stood at 19,000 when Mr. Glocer took the helm②. Meanwhile, it is reducing the number of Reuters' products from 1,300 to about 50, consolidating its global operations around regional hubs③ and raising more than £490m from the sale of non-core businesses.

The process of what Mr. Glocer calls "cultural change" will extend. It is a balancing act that he defines as "a process of not killing the good things about Reuters". Nevertheless, Mr. Glocer agrees that Reuters is approaching a new chapter. "I think a lot of what we have been doing over the last couple of years has really been about fixing the core Reuters

---

① bloated ['bləutid] *adj.* 发胀的
② helm [helm] *n.* 舵
③ hub [hʌb] *n.* 中心

最后一年，这份交易声明也即将面世。 格洛瑟先生的重组计划就是众所周知的"快进"方案。 投资者和客户持鼓励的观点。 伦敦投资银行的证券分析师兼股票经纪人保罗·理查指出，"重要的举措已经完成，投资者认为路透社已经大体上恢复了元气。 他们觉得格洛瑟做得很不错，他们期待金融服务的恢复和路透社的发展能够加速"。

路透社已经超前实现了自己的目标，削减了4.4亿英镑的开支，在1.6万个职位的基础上裁减了3千，格洛瑟先生走马上任之时，公司员工达1.9万名。 同时，它将路透社的产品种类从1 300减少到50左右，巩固了它在各个地区中心的全球性业务，使非核心业务销售额提高到4.9亿多英镑。

格洛瑟先生称之为"文化变革"的过程将会持续延伸。 这是一种平衡的行为，他将其定义为"不让路透社的美好事物毁灭的过程"。 不过，格洛瑟先生承认，路透社正在进入一个新时代。"我认为，我们在过去两年中一直在做的很多事情已经实际上修复了路透社的核心业务，创造了一个发展的平台。 人们在询问下一步合情合理的做法是什么。"他回答这些问题时很委婉，但是重组是一个更集中、更有序的方法，这种模式能给银行、基金管理者和其他财务机构提供市场信息。

路透社的最好产品是3000Xtra信息终端。 这个终端连接跨市场的数据，为交易者、分析员、货币管理者和经济学家提供逻辑分析、绘图功能和新闻。 另一个终端是路透社的Dealing 3000，它是交易员最大的高阶路由网路通道之一。 路透社以这种方式细分市场，尝试给特别的顾客定制产品。 格洛瑟先生经常将这种方式与宝

business and creating a platform for growth, " he says. "It's fair for people to ask what is the next step." He is coy[①] about answering this but the restructuring suggests a much more focused and organized approach to providing banks, fund managers and other financial institutions with market information.

Reuters' number one product is the 3000Xtra information terminal. This combines cross-market data with analytics, charting capabilities and news for traders, analysts, money managers and economists. Another terminal is the Reuters Dealing 3000, which gives traders access to one of the largest order routing networks. By segmenting the market in this way, Reuters attempts to tailor its products for particular customers — in much the same way that BMW, the German car manufacturer, offers a 3, 5 and 7 series for different types of customers, an analogy Mr. Glocer often makes.

There are some observers who wonder whether such segmentation will simply promote market cannibalization, as existing customers switch to lower-priced products. "We've not seen any significant effect of this, " says Mr. Glocer. "What's difficult to measure is this: ' Are there new sales which might have otherwise gone to Xtra but which instead went to Trader?' If there were no cannibalization at all, then we wouldn't have made the middle tier product good enough. The thing is to get your segmentation right enough so that, as a whole, the company is better off having a 7, 5 and 3 series rather than just a 7 and a 3." Underlying the new product range has been a drive to improve its customer service and after-sales support — an area where Bloomberg has traditionally

---

① coy [kɔi] *adj.* 腼腆的

马汽车公司对比，这位德国汽车制造商为不同的顾客提供 3、5、7
型系列。 两家公司的做法大致相同。

有些观察者怀疑，这样的市场细分是否只会促进市场争夺，因
为现有顾客转向了更低价位的产品。 格洛瑟先生说："我们还不清
楚这种方法的影响力度。 测量效果的难度在于'有另外转向 Xtra、
而不找交易员的新销售额吗？'。 如果完全没有竞争，那么我们就
不可能把中间产品做得足够好。 从总体来说，关键是正确地细分市
场，公司最好拥有 7、5、3 系列，而不是仅仅拥有 7 系列和 3 系
列。"潜在的新产品范围一直是改进客服和售后维护的推动力，这是
彭博社一直做得很成功的一个领域。

顾客注意到一个显著的变化。 私有银行施罗德基金管理有限公
司的董事加里·罗德认为，"从客户的角度来看，观察公司这几年的
发展让人饶有兴趣。 他们如何与现有的和潜在的客户谈话，听一下
他们要说什么和做什么，这些都是值得关注的"。 例如，路透社引
入了一系列的产品，意在表明公司经过数年的恢复元气，面对彭博
社的挑战逐步呈上升趋势。 路透社不仅正式推出了即时通讯服务，
也为资本市场的工作人员提供了新产品。 其中的一款产品针对收入
固定的专业人士。 路透社在圣诞节前宣布，多达 32 万个终端能够
处理固定收益交易。 人们预期财务数据的整个市场今年将增长 2%
到 4%，路透社进入中国和消费者市场的增长会更快。 在这些市场
中，它为个人投资者和职场专家们启动了服务业务。 作为其中的一
部分，它最近推出了一个交互式的网络电视新闻频道，将在美国交
付使用。

然而，在所有的这些变化中，路透社并不打算放弃新闻业务。

triumphed.

Customers note a marked change. "From a client perspective, it has been interesting to watch the developments over the last few years, " says Gary Rhodes, IT director at Schroder & Co, the private bank. "It has been noticeable how they are now talking to the existing and potential client base, listening to what they have to say and acting on it." Reuters has, for instance, introduced a series of products that suggest the company is, after several years of getting back on its feet, finally rising to Bloomberg's challenge. It has launched instant messaging services as well as new products for those working in capital markets. One of these benefits fixed income specialists. Just before Christmas, Reuters announced that as many as 320,000 terminals would be able to handle fixed income trading. The overall market for financial data is expected to grow by between 2 and 4 per cent this year, with more rapid growth expected to come from Reuters' push into China and into the consumer market, where it is launching services for individual investors and business professionals. As part of this, it recently launched an interactive internet TV news channel that will be delivered in the US.

Amid all this change, however, Reuters is not about to abandon its news operation. Although Mr. Glocer has sanctioned[①] Reuters' move from its headquarters on Fleet Street, once the home of many of the great media organizations, he is only too aware of the importance of the journalists to Reuters' brand. As it seeks to differentiate itself from its rivals, the news operation — reaching professionals via special terminals and ordinary consumers via newspapers and broadcasters that rely on the journalists'

---

① sanction ['sæŋkʃən] vt. 核准

格洛瑟先生已经批准了路透社从舰队街总部搬迁的计划。 舰队街曾经是各大媒体机构的聚集地。 格洛瑟先生非常清楚记者对路透社品牌的重要性。 因为它试图区别于竞争对手，所以经由特殊终端到达专业人士、经由记者报道的报纸和广播公司到达普通客户的新闻运营变得越来越重要。

正是由于这个原因，记者们不会遭到裁员的冲击，预期只有大约 4% 的编辑人员受格洛瑟先生重组计划的影响。 但是他们也会被换到世界各地其他新的中心去工作，包括班加罗尔的一个新机构，当地的新闻记者将会报道较小的美国上市公司的情况。

这种做法已经引起了记者们的关注。 全国记者联合会驻伦敦办事处的代表维多利亚·巴雷特说："他们将会后悔海外业务外包的想法。 我们不希望看到质量和路透社的声誉以任何方式降低。 你不能裁员再裁员，指望较少的记者完成同样工作。"格洛瑟先生则为这个海外业务战略辩护："路透社自 1866 年来一直在印度存在，所以它不像我们的一些美国公司，只不过发现了一个电话中心，就尽力使人们听起来好像他们来自堪萨斯州。"

但是这些变化还不仅仅只是涉及品牌。 格洛瑟先生希望发展面向消费者的新闻运营，在路透社夺回彭博社市场份额的过程中，使其具备实实在在的运营优势。

知识链接 🔍

Reuters 路透社。路透社是目前英国最大的通讯社和西方四大通讯社之一。路透社在 128 个国家运行，为报刊、电视台等各式媒体提供各类新闻和金融

reports — will become increasingly important.

It is for this reason that the journalists have been spared the brunt① of the job cuts, with only about 4 per cent of its editorial staff expected to be affected by Mr. Glocer's restructuring program. But they are involved in the transfer of jobs to new hubs around the world, including a new facility in Bangalore where journalists will cover results of smaller US-listed companies.

This has prompted concerns among journalists. "They will come to regret their idea of offshoring and outsourcing," says Victoria Barrett, the London bureau's representative for the National Union of Journalists.

"We don't want to see the quality and Reuters' reputation in any way diminished. You can't cut and cut and expect fewer journalists to cover the same work." Mr. Glocer defends the offshoring strategy. "Reuters has been in India since 1866 — so it is not like we are some American company that has just discovered a call centre and that is trying to make people sound like they're from Kansas."

But the changes are not just about brand. Mr. Glocer is hoping the development of its consumer-facing news operation will give it tangible operational advantages as it tries to claw back② market share from Bloomberg.

(1,226 words)

---

① brunt [brʌnt] *n.* 主要的压力
② claw back 夺回

数据，以迅速、准确享誉国际。另一方面，路透提供工具和平台，例如股价和外币汇率，让交易员可以分析金融数据和管理交易风险。同时，路透的系统让客户可以经由互联网完成买卖，取代电话或是纽约证券交易所的买卖大厅等人工交易方式，它的电子交易服务串联了金融社群。

Bloomberg 彭博新闻社（Bloomberg News）。成立于 1981 年的美国彭博资讯公司，是目前全球最大的财经资讯公司，其前身是美国创新市场系统公司。现在，该公司已经发展成为了集新闻、数据和数据分析为一体的全球性多媒体集团，其金融数据市场的销售收入超越了具有 150 年历史的、世界上最大的资讯公司——路透集团。

题　记

　　在拥有大量机密的硅谷，如果一个羽翼未丰的新兴公司不懂得保护他们的技术机密，那么，很快就会被竞争对手所打败。对于小公司来说，保护机密的工作是容易的，但对于像拥有将近万名员工的苹果电脑这样的大公司来说，就是件很困难的事情了。在硅谷的所有技术公司中，独有苹果公司拥有一大堆专门进行刺探和推断该公司研发动向的网站，而且也只有苹果公司的总裁在演讲的时候，才会像潮水一样涌来一大群狂热的追随者。苹果公司的沉默，归因于他们的保密动机：生存和营销。苹果不愿过多披露其首席执行官史蒂夫·乔布斯的健康信息，其实源于该公司多年来形成的一种"保密文化"。这种保密文化能够在人们心里留下一片空间，增加苹果产品给人们带来的惊喜、兴奋度和神秘感。

Apple's Culture of Secrecy

"A New York newspaper today called into question some issues around Steve and his health. Would you mind addressing the situation?" A Lehman Brothers analyst named Ben Reitzes gently asked.

"Steve loves Apple, " replied Peter Oppenheimer, the company's chief financial officer. "He serves as the C.E.O. at the pleasure of Apple's board and has no plans to leave Apple. Steve's health is a private matter."

That was it. No insistence that he was cancer-free. No attempt to explain his gaunt condition. No nothing. When I spoke to Steve Dowling in Apple's public relations department, I got the same response. "Steve's health is a private matter, " Mr. Dowling said. Then, just for good measure, he said it again. "Steve's health is a private matter."

There are no hard and fast rules about how and when companies need to disclose information about the health of their chief executives. In 1995, when Andrew S. Grove, then the chief executive of Intel, received a diagnosis of prostate cancer, he informed the company's board and management. But he never told the company's shareholders. Mr. Grove says now that because the cancer never impaired① his ability to do his job,

---

① impair [im'peə] *vt.* 损害;削弱

苹果公司的文化机密

　　"一家纽约的报纸今天报道了史蒂夫和他的健康问题。 你们能不能谈谈这方面的情况？" 雷曼兄弟的分析师本·雷特兹优雅地问道。

　　"史蒂夫热爱苹果。 他很高兴担任苹果公司董事会的首席执行官，目前他还没有任何离职计划。 史蒂夫的健康是他的个人私事。"苹果公司的首席财政官彼得·奥本海默回答说。

　　确实如此。 苹果并未坚持认为乔布斯没有患上癌症，但同时也不愿意披露乔布斯的具体病情。 什么都没有做。 我曾向苹果发言人史蒂夫·道林询问乔布斯的健康问题，但道林的回答与奥本海默一模一样。 道林先生说："乔布斯的健康是他的个人私事。"然后，为了安抚大家，他还一再重复："乔布斯的健康是他的个人私事。"

　　企业掌门人是否应该及时公布个人健康状况，并没有硬性的规定。 1995 年，时任英特尔首席执行官的安迪·格罗夫收到了前列腺癌的诊断书，他虽然马上就此通知了英特尔高管层和董事会，但却决定对英特尔的股东们隐瞒该消息。 格罗夫先生认为，癌症并不影响自己的日常工作，因此没有必要向英特尔股东通报相关信息。 人们在一年后根据他写下的病情记载才了解了真相。

there was no reason to inform shareholders. The world found out about Mr. Grove's illness only when he wrote about it the following year.

On the other hand, when Charles H. Bell received a diagnosis of colorectal cancer shortly after he became the chief executive of McDonald's, the company quickly released the news. Mr. Bell resigned from the company immediately, and died two months later.

"The question surrounding any kind of corporate disclosure always is: Is it material?" said Larry S. Gondelman, a lawyer with Powers Pyles Sutter & Verville. "And there is no bright line test in determining materiality." A spokesman for the Securities and Exchange Commission said that the law defined materiality as information that "the reasonable investor needs to know in order to make an informed decision about his investment."

No company has ever been held to account by the S.E.C. for failing to disclose information about its chief executive's health, and I'm not suggesting that the S.E.C. should go after Apple for keeping mum about Mr. Jobs's health. Indeed, I found plenty of people who felt he had every right to keep the information to himself. "As long as he is healthy, he doesn't have to disclose," said Charles R. Wolf, an analyst at Needham & Company. Roger McNamee, the well-known technology investor at Elevation Partners, said, "Because Steve Jobs has been appearing in public regularly, investors are getting a valuable form of disclosure."

But if ever there was a chief executive who ought to feel some responsibility to tell shareholders about his health, it is Steve Jobs. First of all, he is not like other chief executives — he is, instead, the single most indispensable chief executive on the planet. As Mr. Wolf nicely put

与此相反的是，查尔斯·贝尔担任麦当劳的行政长官不久，就收到了直肠癌诊断书。麦当劳很快对外公布了该消息。贝尔先生随即向公司辞职，并于两个月后去世。

鲍尔斯·帕勒斯·萨特·维韦勒律师事务所的律师拉里·古德尔曼对此表示："大家对企业所通报的任何信息通常担心的是：这些信息是否真实？在确定真实性方面没有明确实用的标准。"美国证券交易委员会一位发言人表示，法律将信息的重要性定义为"理性的投资者需要知道企业的信息，以便做出明智的投资决断"。

美国证券交易委员会从不追究公司不披露公司首席执行官的健康状况的责任，但我不是说美国证券交易委员应当和苹果公司一样对乔布斯的健康状况保持缄默。事实上，我发现大部分人都觉得自己有权保护自己的隐私。美国投资机构李约瑟公司的分析师查尔斯·沃尔夫对此表示："只要乔布斯能够正常工作，他就没有必要披露他的健康信息。"著名的高地风险投资公司的科技投资人罗杰·麦克纳米认为，"既然乔布斯仍然定期在公开场合露面，投资者可将其视为珍贵的信息披露"。

但是，如果真有一位首席执行官感到有责任向股东透露他的健康信息，那肯定非乔布斯莫属。首先，乔布斯与普通的首席执行官不同。当然，他不是这个地球上最不可缺少的行政长官。但正如沃尔夫先生恰到好处的点评："苹果就是乔布斯，乔布斯就是苹果。"他还说："如果乔布斯哪天意外地离职，我敢打赌，苹果当天股价肯定会下跌 25% 或以上。"当投资者低声谈论乔布斯的健康状况时，这并不是他们喜欢这些闲言碎语，而是因为乔布斯的健康状况确实关乎苹果的未来。

it, "Apple is Steve Jobs and Steve Jobs is Apple." He added, "I think the stock would drop 25 percent or more if he were to leave the company unexpectedly." When investors whisper about Mr. Jobs's health, it's not just gossip they are indulging in — his health really matters to Apple's future.

Secondly, Mr. Jobs has had cancer, and in the public mind, a particularly insidious① kind. Although several doctors I spoke to say that the kind of cancer he had, and the kind of operation he underwent, give him a better-than-even chance of living a long and happy life, there are no guarantees with cancer. We all know that. Which is all the more reason why, at a minimum, Apple should flatten the rumor that his cancer has recurred — even if it won't go further than that. "Not being able to provide a statement effectively dismissing the question is really unsatisfactory to most investors, " said A. M. Sacconaghi Jr., who follows the company for Sanford C. Bernstein.

The final reason, to be blunt② about it, is that Apple simply can't be trusted to tell truth about its chief executive. Under Mr. Jobs, Apple has created a culture of secrecy that has served it well in many ways — the speculation over which products Apple will unveil at the annual MacWorld conference has been one of the company's best marketing tools. But that same culture poisons its corporate governance. Apple tells analysts far less about its operations than most companies do. It turns low-level decisions into state secrets. Directors are often left out of the loop. And it

---

① insidious [in'sidiəs] *adj.* 阴险的;隐伏的
② blunt [blʌnt] *adj.* 钝的;直率的

其次，乔布斯已身患癌症，在公众心目中，它是一种具有潜伏期的癌症。虽然与我交谈过的几位医生表示，乔布斯身患的这种癌症以及他经历的癌症手术会让他活得更久和更快乐，但在癌症问题上，谁也不敢打包票。我们都知道这一点。所有这些使人更有理由认为，为什么苹果至少应该平静地对待乔布斯的癌症复发的传闻，即使谣言还不至于达到那种地步。市场研究公司桑福德·C.伯恩斯坦的分析师 A. M.萨康纳吉认为，"在乔布斯癌症是否复发问题上，苹果的高管层避而不答，股东们自然会感到不满"。

坦率地讲，苹果公司如果说出了首席执行官身患癌症的实情，就会完全丧失投资者的信任，这就是最后一个原因。在乔布斯的领导下，苹果已创建了一种保密文化，这种保密文化在很多方面为苹果服务。苹果将在年度 MacWorld 大会上推出哪些产品，这种猜测已成为公司的最佳营销工具之一。但是，这种保密文化也给公司管理造成了负面影响。与大多数公司相比，苹果对分析师透露的公司运营信息要少得多。它将低层决定变为国家机密。苹果董事会的成员也常被排斥在圈外。苹果正在泰然自若地隐瞒真相。

就像人们所说的，这个事件确实出现了最新的插曲。约翰·马科夫在《纽约时报》撰文称，乔布斯今年早些时候又做了一次外科手术，但具体详情不得而知。我听说，乔布斯患了消化类疾病或是手术后遗症，这些困难导致他体重减轻。在会议前的几个星期，手术感染使他看起来很憔悴。谢天谢地，这不是癌症。但是，这又不仅仅是一个"常见的疾病"。如果乔布斯果真是癌症复发，而苹果又不愿公布该消息，那么苹果公司就是在欺骗股东。

乔布斯要真是癌症复发那就太可怕了。我希望这种事永远也不

dissembles with impunity.

As, indeed, it has in this latest episode. John Markoff reported in The New York Times that Mr. Jobs had had a surgical procedure earlier this year, the details of which remain unclear. I hear that he has had ongoing digestive difficulties, which have contributed to his weight loss — possibly a side effect of the surgery. And in the weeks leading up to the conference, he came down with an infection, which had a lot to do with why he looked so gaunt①. It wasn't cancer, thank goodness. But it was more than a "common bug." By claiming Mr. Jobs had a bug, Apple wasn't just going dark on its shareholders. It was deceiving them.

It would be horrible if Mr. Jobs had a recurrence of cancer. I hope it never happens. At 53, he is in the prime of his life, the father of a young family. And for the rest of us, it's exhilarating② watching him work his magic in the marketplace. Steve Jobs has created more value and driven more innovation than just about anybody in business. Who doesn't want to see what he'll come up with next?

He also, though, needs to treat his shareholders with at least a modicum③ of respect. And telling them whether or not he is sick would be a good place to start. You would think he'd want them to know before me. But apparently not.

(995 words)

---

① gaunt [gɔːnt] *adj.* 憔悴的；枯瘦的
② exhilarating [ig'ziləreitiŋ] *adj.* 使人愉快的；令人喜欢的
③ modicum ['mɔdikəm] *n.* 少量，一点点

152

要发生。 53 岁的乔布斯正处在人生的巅峰时期，是一个年轻家庭的父亲。 对我们其他人来说，看他在市场上施展魔力令人愉悦。 史蒂夫·乔布斯比其他商界人士创造了更多的价值，推动了更多的创新。 谁不想看看接下来他又会创造什么呢？

但是，他至少也得给他的股民们一点点尊重。 不论他生病与否，都应该开诚布公地告诉股东，这将是一个良好的开端。 你会觉得他可能想当着我的面向股东公布实情。 但显然不是。

知识链接

Elevation Partners 高地风险投资公司。高地是硅谷的一家私募股权公司，公司的专长是针对市场领先的消费与技术企业进行大规模投资。高地投资从客户的角度出发，充分理解客户的财富管理需求，为客户提供广阔的投资视野，客户可以自由地选择银行、证券、基金、信托、保险、私募股权等各类跨行业的金融投资产品。高地投资还有专业的团队对金融产品进行跟踪管理，及时与客户沟通最新的产品情况及风险提示，确保客户的投资资产稳健、安全、增长。摇滚乐队 U2 的成员波诺（Bono）是这家公司的董事合伙人，麦克奈米是高地风险投资公司的创始人。

题　记

　　酒店价格与服务的性价比往往是酒店谈判的焦点。酒店谈判即使没有唇枪舌剑、兵戎相见的火药味，但谈判过程中的技巧和原则却为后期的成功奠定了基础。打电话到酒店预订房间前应该先行调查，做到知己知彼方能百战不殆。寻找合理报价时，只与当事主管谈判，把握"能说会道"的节奏和攻心为上的"度"。将相关意见以恰当的方式反馈给酒店管理人员，通过主动协商获得最大权益。跟踪预定信息，以不变应万变。记下所有遇到的员工的名字，在需要帮助时向他们求助。如果有未解决的投诉，写信给饭店经理或总裁。友好、尊重、不卑不亢会让人感觉无限温暖，从而和酒店以及酒店的管理人员建立一定的信任和友好的关系。

How to Negotiate with a Hotel

1. Do Your Research

When you call a hotel to make a reservation, you should already have done your research. You should already have checked the online rate. Since there are no humans involved, the rate is often lower. You can also get commentary online with websites such as TripAdvisor or recommendations from guide books. Find out how many stars it has. When you do ask for the rate, find out what discounts you can use, including Senior of Auto Club discount or other loyalty clubs. Ask if there are any weekend or special rates. When given the rate, ask if they are any lower rates available. Call more than once to see if you get different quotes. If you see an offer that seems too good to be true, book it immediately because it probably will not be there the next time you try.

2. Only Negotiate with Someone with Authority

When looking for a good rate, it is usually better to deal directly with the front desk instead of online or through the hotels web sites. Individual hotel managers have authority to be more flexible in their rates, especially later in the day. Heads in beds are better than an empty bed. The online rates usually cannot be altered. You should also check rates at nearby hotels and comparable hotels. If you are not quoted a good

如何与酒店谈判

1. 做调查

打电话到酒店预订房间前应该先做调查。 起码应该查看酒店的网上报价。 因为无人入住，网上的报价往往较低。 还可以上 **TripAdvisor** 等旅游网站查看在线评论，或者从旅游指南类书籍中获得一些建议。 查看酒店是几星级的。 查找网上报价时，看看你能享受什么样的折扣。 包括询问是汽车俱乐部还是其他高档俱乐部的高级会员。 问问看有没有周末报价或其他特价。 别人给你报价时，问一下还有没有更低的价格。 多打几次电话，看看会不会得到不同的报价。 如果你看到某个报价便宜得难以置信，立即预订，否则你下次再问的时候可能就没有这么优惠的价格了。

2. 只与当事主管谈判

寻找合理报价时，直接与前台交涉通常比在线或者通过酒店的网站交流要好。 个别酒店的经理有权进一步盘活价格，尤其是当天的晚些时候。 入住率比空床位更有利。 网上的报价通常是不能更改的。 你也可以去附近或者是同等的酒店核查价格。 得不到好的报价，不妨报出其竞争对手的价格。 要显示出一副随时走人的架势，如果必要的话就去别家酒店。

rate, you can point out what their competitors' rates are. Show that you are prepared to walk away and go next door if necessary.

If you have a problem or issue after you have checked into a hotel, go to the front desk and ask to see the manager. Again, this is usually the only person who can waive① policies and do something for you such as a free night or an upgrade for the inconvenience you may have suffered for a noisy or a dirty room.

3. If You Don't Ask, You Don't Get

I think this is the most important rule. My mother says, "The worst thing that can happen is that they say 'no'." First you have to ask the right questions. "Is this the best you can do?" "Do you have any specials?" Can you give me an upgrade? You don't really have to have a problem to ask for something better. I was traveling with my son, his wife, my grandson and my dog. Our room at a chain hotel had one bed, one pull-out couch and one bathroom. I knew we were going to be cramped② and I probably should have booked two separate rooms. I went to the front desk and told them the situation and they gave me a suite which had two bathrooms and two bedrooms with a sitting area for the same cost. Everyone was more comfortable and we will always have good feelings about that chain. It was definitely a win-win result.

4. Keep Track of the Paperwork

Once you get your reservation, get the name of the reservationist and the reservation number. If you made your reservation via phone, ask them to send you an email so you have the proof to take with you. If someone

---

① waive [weiv] *vt.* 放弃
② cramp [kræmp] *vt.* 使拥挤

158

如果入住酒店之后有麻烦或问题，直接到前台求见经理。 同样，经理通常是唯一可以灵活使用规则、为你解决困难的人，如果你入住的房间嘈杂脏乱，他可以免除你今晚的房费，或者给你换更好的房间。

3. 主动要求才会获得利益

我认为这是最重要的规则。 我的母亲认为，"可能发生的、最糟糕的事情就是他们说'不'"。 首先，你要问正确的问题："这就是你们能做到的最好的吗？""你们有什么特色服务？""你能给我更好的房间吗？"你不必非得找出酒店的问题再寻求更好的服务。 有一次，我和儿子、儿媳、孙子及我的狗一起旅行。 我们在一家连锁酒店订的房间有一张床，一个可以拉开放平的沙发和一个浴室。 如果我早知道会如此拥挤，我就会订两间房。 我去了前台，告诉他们这种情况，他们以同样的价格为我们换了一个有两个卫生间和两间卧室及客厅的套房。 每个人都感到很舒适，而且这家连锁酒店给我们留下了永远美好的印象。 这肯定是一个双赢的结果。

4. 跟踪预订信息

一旦预订成功，要留下预约人的名字和预约号码。 如果你用电话预订，要求他们给你发送一封电子邮件，这样你就能随身携带证据。 如果需要他人帮你预订，如面试，一定要提前打电话，确认预订成功。 我曾经遇到过这样的事：我预订的酒店因为公司没有确认而被取消，幸好他们还有一间空房。 但现在我总是会提前打电话，确保预订万无一失。 也可以利用这个信息查看价格是否已经发生了变化。 如果价格已经降低，要求降价或取消现有的预订，重新预约。

else is making the reservation for you, such as a job interview, always call ahead and make sure the reservation is confirmed. I had this happen to me. The hotel reservation had been cancelled because the company had not confirmed the reservation. Luckily they had a room available, but now I always call ahead and make sure the reservation is still good. You can also use this information to see if the rate has changed. If the rate is lower, ask for a reduction or cancel the existing reservation and make a new one.

5. Write Down the Names of all Staff Encountered

This may sound a little paranoid, but sometimes something will be noticed after you have left the hotel and knowing the names of the hotel employees will be crucial. I stayed in a hotel one summer and discovered four hours after checking out that the valet① who parked our van had scraped the top of the van in the garage facility without letting anyone know. I only noticed it because we were parked at a rest stop two hundred miles away and looked down at the van and noticed the damage. At that point, I contacted the hotel and explained the situation. It really helped that I had the name of the valet who had driven the car. We had even given him a tip that morning because we did not have cash earlier. I asked how to file a complaint and who to contact. I was given the Human Resources representative who had their insurance rep call us. When I got the online survey, I put all the information about the damage to the car and our disappointment that an employee would not inform us about the damage. We got an estimate over $ 1,000 and luckily their insurance company paid it. If we did not have the name of the employee, I am not

---

① valet ['vælit] *n.* 泊车小弟

5. 记下所有遇到的员工的名字

这种做法可能听起来有点偏执，但有时在你离开酒店之后才发现一些问题，所以了解酒店员工的名字将至关重要。 有一年夏天，我住在一家酒店，付账离开 4 个小时后，才发现帮我们泊车的服务生在停车场里刮坏了车顶，但他没有告诉任何人。 我也是在 200 英里外的一个休息站停车时，从车顶往下看才注意到了这个刮痕。 当时，我联系了酒店，并解释了有关情况。 我知道帮我们泊车的服务生的名字，这真是帮了我们大忙。 因为之前我们没有现金，那天早上我们还给了他小费。 我询问酒店如何投诉和与谁联系，得到人力资源部代理人的联系方式，他让保险公司的人打电话给我们。 当我接受在线调查时，我上传了所有关于汽车损坏的信息，并表达了员工对我们隐瞒划痕的失望。 汽车估计受损超过 1 千美元，幸运的是，他们的保险公司支付了这笔费用。 如果我们不知道那位员工的名字，我不敢肯定我们会得到这样的结果。

6. 如果有未解决的投诉，写信给饭店经理或总裁

在酒店遇到的任何问题都要详细记录下来，包括到底出了什么错，什么时候出的错，出错时帮助你的员工的姓名，以及没有帮你解决问题的员工的姓名。 这一点非常重要。 如果事情发生时不把这些细节记下来，过后就会很模糊。 如果你没有时间把一切都写下来，可以在回家的飞机上做这个工作，总之尽快。 以后如果你决定投诉或写信给主管，这些信息会有帮助。 如果你提供的事实详尽，时间准确，申诉信就会非常有说服力。

许多酒店尽职尽责地面向客户服务，欢迎客户多提意见。 有些酒店甚至会向你发送在线调查，询问你的住宿情况。 如果有问题，

sure we would have the same result.

6. Write a Letter to the Hotel Manager or CEO if There are Unresolved Complaints

If there are any problems at the hotel, keep copious① notes of what went wrong, when it went wrong, and the names of the employees who helped you and those who did not help you resolve it. This is very important because those details can be very fuzzy② if you do not write them down when the incident happens. If you don't have time to write it all down, do it on your flight home or as soon as possible. This will help you later on if you decide to file a complaint or write a letter to the president. Your letter will be very professional if you have all your facts and times straight.

Many hotels are very customer service oriented and welcome comments. Some will even send you an online survey to ask how your stay was. If there were problems, this is a good opportunity to say why you were upset and what you would like to remedy the situation. If you don't get a survey, send a letter to the Hotel Manager with exactly what happened. Be sure to say what you want. If you don't get an answer, send a letter to the CEO of the company. If you follow these rules, you will be Negotiating like a Professional.

(1,082 words)

---

① copious [ˈkəupiəs] *adj.* 详细的
② fuzzy [ˈfʌzi] *adj.* 模糊的

这是一个发表意见的好机会，可以诉说你为什么感到心烦意乱，对发生的情况你想如何补救。 如果你没有接受调查，可以写信给饭店经理，告诉他具体发生了什么事。 明确地说出你想要怎么样。 如果你没有得到回复，写信给公司的首席执行官。 如果你遵循这些规则，就可以像专业人士一样与他们谈判。

知识链接 🔍

TripAdvisor Tripadvisor. com 是全球最大、最受欢迎的旅游社区，也是全球第一的旅游评论网站。月访问量达3 500万人，同时拥有超过1 000万的注册会员以及2 500多万条的评论，并且数量还在不断增加中。旅行者的真实评论是 TripAdvisor 最大的特点。TripAdvisor 在美国、英国、西班牙、印度、中国等地都设有分站，总共包含了全球超过400 000家酒店和90 000个景点的信息介绍。总体来说，TripAdvisor 的媒体网络已经在世界范围内的媒体圈获得了数以百计的奖项和赞美。TripAdvisor 以及其媒体网站现在隶属于美国大型旅游公司艾派迪公司(Expedia Inc.) 。

题　记

　　漫长的求职过程往往使应聘者签下一家公司后如释重负，他们根本没有考虑招聘方是否会利用信息不对称的强势压缩薪资谈判空间。几乎所有人都会认为薪酬谈判的动机再简单不过——争取更好的薪酬待遇。其实薪酬谈判和打扑克没有什么两样，雇主并没有使出浑身的解数，总是有更多的回旋余地。掌握一些谈判的小技巧，会为薪酬谈判增加几分胜算：不要把工资底线降得太低；对自己的工作能力要适当估量；适时展现自己的潜能；不轻易地讲出自己的薪水要求；在还未摸清薪酬水平的可能变动幅度之前就突兀地把自己推销出去等同冒险。人们常常将职业视作领取薪酬的支票，实际上，它的价值远高于这一切。

The Worth of Your Paycheck

What a relief! The grueling① task of finding a job is over. You received an offer, and the company presented you with your starting salary and benefits package.

But wait. Before you hastily agree to the terms and sign on the dotted line, do some homework to find out if you're being offered a competitive salary. If not — or even if you need a few thousand dollars more to cover the rent — negotiate. It's something recent grads are reluctant to do since they're often grateful just to be hired. After all, it's not as if they have a wealth of on the job experience. It's great to be appreciative and enthusiastic, but don't forget: not only can you negotiate the salary of your first job, you should.

Here's one reason why: "It's no different than how we play poker②," says Michael Ball, founder of Career Freshman, a California-based company that teaches employers how to manage recent graduates.

"Employers are not coming in with their full hand. So, there's always more wiggle③ room." Chris Fusco, vice president of compensation at

---

① grueling [ˈgruəliŋ] *n.* 残酷的
② poker [ˈpəukə] *n.* 纸牌戏
③ wiggle [ˈwigl] *n.* 浮动

薪酬的价值

　　终于松了一口气！ 找工作的劳顿烟消云散。 你收到一份雇佣合同，公司承诺给你起薪并享受福利套餐。

　　请等等。 在你匆忙答应合同条款、在虚线上签名之前，请先弄清楚公司是否为你提供了优厚的薪酬。 如果还没有，一定要与之协商，因为你还需要几千美元付房租。 这是刚毕业的大学生不愿意做的事，只要能够被聘用，他们就感激涕零。 毕竟，他们似乎还缺乏丰富的工作经历。 懂得珍惜和富有热情是再好不过的事，但请记住：你不仅可以与雇主协商第一份工作的薪水，也应该如此去做。

　　总部设在加利福尼亚的职场新人公司的创始人迈克尔·波尔，指出了出现这种状况的一个原因，他在指导员工如何管理刚毕业的大学生时声称："管理新人和打扑克其实没有什么两样。 雇主并没有使出全身的解数，所以，总是有更多的回旋余地。" 薪水网负责赔偿事宜的副总裁查理斯·福斯科认为，谈判结果通常"比初始薪水上浮 10% 左右"。 他建议可以这样说："基于我对这份工作的理解、公司的需要以及我所拥有的技能与经验，我认为我所能提供的价值比你给我的工资高出 5 000 美元。"

　　福斯科建议，毕业生应该让雇主意识到自己过去的工作或实习

Salary.com says negotiating often results in "about 10% improvement on the initial offer." He recommends saying something like "Based on my understanding of the job, the company's needs, and the skills and experience I bring, I feel I'm worth $ 5,000 more than what you're offering me."

Fusco advises students to make employers aware of the work and internship experience they've had in the past, recommendations from professors and former employers, and details of extracurricular activities, to show the strong potential they have for success at the company. If the thought of negotiating for a few thousand dollars more makes you queasy①, consider this: Annual raises are usually a percentage of your salary. "That incremental negotiation you do at the front end continues to pay you back when it's time for a percentage raise, " says Ball. It goes on from there, especially if you're at the company for several years.

That's particularly true for women. Among employees who work full time and are one year out of college, females are making only 80% of what their male counterparts earn, according to a new study by the American Association of University Women. Granted, there are variables at play, such as the jobs women chose, education received and whether they work at a for-profit company versus a nonprofit or governmental organization. But when Catherine Hill, director of research at the association and co-author of the report "Behind the Pay Gap, " accounted for those variables statistically, there was still a 5% difference between men and women that's not explained. Women's lack of

---

① queasy ['kwiːzi] *adj.* 使人呕吐的

经历，让他们了解教授和先前雇主的推荐信，课外活动的细节，以显示自己在公司有获得成功的巨大潜力。 如果你觉得为了区区几千美元讨价还价于心不安，可以这么想：每年薪水的增长量不过是薪水的百分之一。 波尔认为，"你之前做的增值性薪水谈判将使你一到加薪水的时候就受益"。 它将从一个更高的薪水起点开始计算，尤其是你打算在这个公司干上几年。

对于职场女性而言更是如此。 美国大学女性协会的最新调查显示，那些刚从大学毕业一年、从事全职工作的雇员中，女性的薪水只相当于同等条件男性的80%。 当然，还有变量在起作用，例如女性的就业选择、接受教育的水平以及她们是为盈利性公司工作还是为非盈利公司或政府机构工作。 但是美国大学女性协会的主编、《薪资差距的真实原因》报告的合作撰稿人凯瑟琳·希尔用数据解释了这些变量，但是还有5%的男女薪资差距依旧无法解释。 她认为，这与女性缺乏谈判技巧有关。

谈判也许会带来额外的好处，这一点男性和女性都应该谙熟于心。 福斯科说："一个有前途的员工的谈判方式充分地反映了此人在未来工作岗位上的表现。 他们是否可以影响他人采取行动，他们是否能够通过游说获取资源，均可以此为鉴。 无论你做什么，都不要告诉招聘人员你的期望值。 这是个下下之策。 如果你要价太高，无异于搬起石头砸自己的脚；但如果要价过低，又会在经济上给自己造成损失。 如果被问起对薪水的期望，最好的回答莫过于："能为本公司效力我感到十分荣幸，并且我也相信凭我的能力完全可以为公司做出相应的贡献。 我确信，我们在薪水上能达成一致，双方都会感到满意。"

negotiating skills likely has something to do with it, she says.

Both genders should keep in mind that negotiating might have another benefit. "How a prospective employee negotiates is a good indicator of how that person will perform on the job," says Fusco. "It's an indicator of whether they'll be able to influence others to take action and if they can lobby to get resources." Whatever you do, don't tell the recruiter how much you hope to make. It's a lose-lose situation. If you ask for too much, you can price yourself out of the job, but if you ask for too little, you're hurting yourself financially. If asked, the right thing to say is, "I'm very excited about working for this company, and I think I have a lot to bring. I'm sure we can work together to agree on salary that suits both of us."

Never go into raise negotiations without knowing what other people in your profession are making. The first place to check is your university's career center. Career counselors can tell you if the company's salary history is consistent with its offer. From there, ask if the recruiter can put you in touch with last year's grads who received offers from that company and their competitors. If you're planning to negotiate, ask the contact how he or she negotiated and if it was successful. That person can also offer tips on how to ask for more money since he or she knows the company's culture after being there for a year. Then, see what recent grads with similar jobs in your geographic area are making by visiting sites like salary.com and vault.com. These sites post all sorts of information from employees about what it's like to work for their organization.

Many companies hire entry-level employees into structured programs that give them an opportunity to rotate throughout the company. Salaries for those positions aren't usually flexible. That doesn't mean there isn't

当你不知道其他同事的薪资水平时，决不要开启薪资谈判的大门。 了解薪资的第一选择就是拜访你就读大学的就业中心。 职业咨询师会告诉你，公司给你的薪酬是否符合历史水平。 你可以在就业中心询问招聘人员，能否通过他们与去年收到该公司和其他竞争公司录用通知的毕业生联系上。 如果你打算就薪资进行谈判，询问你联系上的人，他们是如何谈判的，是否取得了成功。 这个人也可以传授一些小建议，告诉你如何获得更高的薪资，因为他们在公司待了一年之后，已经熟悉了公司的文化。 随后，访问薪资网和保险库网等网站，了解在相关领域内从事类似工作、刚毕业的大学生的薪资水平。 这些网站发布各种各样的信息，雇员们在上面交流各自机构的工作状况。

很多公司制定了结构化的程序，刚入职的员工有机会在整个公司轮岗。 这些岗位的工资通常缺乏灵活性。 泰科国际的人事主管维多利亚·特雷西认为，即使如此，也还存在着协商的空间。 她建议双方开诚布公。 例如，如果你需要公司帮你解决搬家费，你可以告诉招聘人员，这笔钱能否以签约奖金的形式发放。

询问你的上级主管，能否按半年而不是一年的时间来评价你的工作绩效，特雷西认为这是另一种获得结构性薪酬的方法。 她说："我们希望，那些为我们工作的应征人员一进公司就感觉良好。 我们也希望他们保持理智。 如果他们愿意和我们一道工作，我们很乐意了解他们所关心的事情。"

记住，有些工作实在是太好了，即使工资不能按时发放，也难以拒绝。 当涉及专业发展和工作与生活之间的平衡时，教会你绝技的项目或拥有辉煌业绩的雇主确实让人欲罢不能。 有些工作和雇主

room for discussion, says Victoria Tracy, director of staffing at Tyco International. She recommends being completely honest. For instance, if you need help with moving costs, she suggests telling the recruiter to see if that money can be put in the form of a signing bonus.

Another way to get around a structured salary is to ask if your manager can review your performance and salary at six months instead of at the year mark, she says. "We want candidates who work for us to feel good as soon as they walk in the door, " says Tracy. "We also want them to be reasonable. If they're willing to work with us, we're willing to listen to their concerns."

Keep in mind that some offers are too good to refuse even if the money isn't there. That's true for programs that will teach you unique skills or employers that have exemplary① records when it comes to professional development and work/life balance. Some jobs and employers are so prestigious that having it on your ré sumé will help you get other, more lucrative② offers. "Too often people see their career as nothing but a paycheck, " says John Leech, director of recruitment for FedEx. "It really is so much more."

Tyco's Tracy offers one final piece of advice: No matter what, never, ever have your parents call up to do the negotiating for you.

(1,000 words)

----

① exemplary [ig'zempləri] *adj.* 可仿效的
② lucrative ['lju:krətiv] *adj.* 有利益的

声名显赫，写进你的简历可以帮你得到另外一份更高报酬的工作。联邦快递的招聘理事约翰·里奇认为，"人们常常将职业视作领取薪酬的支票，实际上，它的价值远高于这一切"。

泰科公司的特雷西最后提出了一个忠告：不管发生什么事，永远不要让父母给公司打电话商讨你的薪酬。

知识链接 🔍

FedEx Express 联邦快递。联邦快递隶属于美国联邦快递集团（FedEx Corp.），是集团快递运输业务的中坚力量。联邦快递是全球最具规模的快递运输公司，设有环球航空及陆运网络，为超过 235 个国家及地区的顾客和企业提供涵盖运输、电子商务和商业运作等一系列快捷、可靠的全面服务。联邦快递集团激励旗下超过 2.6 万名员工和承包商高度关注安全问题，恪守品行道德和职业操守的最高标准，并尽最大努力满足客户和社会的需求，使其屡次被评为全球最受尊敬和最可信赖的雇主。

题　记

　　肯德基、麦当劳和必胜客在中国早已是家喻户晓的洋快餐品牌，其舒适的环境、周到的服务、良好的卫生条件以及统一的包装深受中国消费者的青睐。这些外国快餐店在中国占据了很大的市场份额，增长势头非常强劲，造成了对中国传统快餐的巨大冲击。尽管人们喜欢在上班路上狼吞虎咽，休闲时喝杯可乐放松放松，但品种相对单一，与中国人的传统饮食习惯不一致等问题，也造成了这些快餐企业发展的"瓶颈"。美国百胜全球餐饮集团在上海肯德基连锁店率先推出了传统的北京鸡肉卷，肯德基在菜单中增加了四川榨菜和肉丝汤，麦当劳不甘落后，推出了蔬菜海鲜汤和玉米汤。这种卓越的跨文化管理模式既是市场经济发展的产物，也体现了人类与现代生活快节奏的和解。

A Model of Blended Culture
of Foreign Fast Foods

CEOs of America Tricon Global Restaurants, the group that owns KFC and Pizza Hut, promotes Traditional Peking Chicken Roll at a KFC restaurant in Shanghai. At present, there are numerous KFC restaurants in China, and they are increasing at annual rate of 200. A new KFC restaurant opens every other day. Western counterpart McDonald's also continues to expand its premises.

Having arrived on the mainland in the early 1990s, McDonald's has so many restaurants in nearly 100 cities. Although there have been fewer golden arches in America, its native country, in the past two years, China's McDonald's have grown at a rate of 100 restaurants per year.

The total income of fast food restaurants in China now stands at 180 billion Yuan RMB, and KFC and McDonald's account for eight percent. What kind of magic has brought them such success in China? How do they sustain growth rates? Their standardized business operation apart, the key is excellent inter-cultural management.

Western Fast Food — Chinese Style

Alluring the captious① customers is a hurdle every foreign fast food

---

① captious[ˈkæpʃəs] *adj.* 吹毛求疵的

洋快餐的混合文化模式

美国百胜全球餐饮集团的执行总裁们在上海肯德基连锁店推出了传统的北京鸡肉卷。该集团旗下拥有肯德基和必胜客两大品牌。中国目前有无数家肯德基餐厅，并且这个数字还在以每年 200 的速度飙升。每隔一天都会有一家新的肯德基开业。其西方对手麦当劳也在继续拓展疆土。

麦当劳自 20 世纪 90 年代登陆中国大陆以来，已经在将近 100 座城市里拥有很多家餐厅。尽管在美国本土没有那么多金黄色的双拱门，但在过去两年里，中国的麦当劳以每年 100 家的速度递增。

中国快餐行业的总收入每年大约 1 800 亿人民币，其中麦当劳和肯德基占 8% 。他们在中国如此成功的秘诀是什么？它们为何能持续增长？标准化经营之外，关键是其卓越的跨文化管理。

西方快餐——中国风格

每家洋快餐厅都必须吸引挑剔的顾客。新奇的快餐店一开始就会赢得许多顾客。尽管这些洋快餐在美国本土既便宜又普通，但在中国政府刚刚实施对外开放政策的时候，快餐富有的异国情调足以激起中国人对外面世界的好奇。快餐店的经理们借此优势制定了相对昂

restaurant must clear. The novelty of these fast food restaurants initially won many customers. Although cheap and commonplace in America, at the time the Chinese government's opening-up policy was newly enacted, fast food was exotically foreign enough to whet① Chinese people's curiosity about the outside world. Managers took advantage of this by charging the relatively high prices of 10 Yuan for a hamburger, and 5 Yuan for a Coke.

By the mid-1990s, there were 100 fast food restaurants around Beijing; the convenience, efficient service, comfortable environment, pleasing music and jovial② atmosphere garnered fans. Office workers enjoyed grabbing a quick bite on their way to work, and friends enjoyed relaxing over a Coke. However, certain eagle-eyed managers noticed that some people never dropped in when they passed by. Some customers complained that fast food was not as good as their Chinese cuisine, and that it lacked variety. McDonald's and KFC restaurants were almost empty during the traditional celebrations of Spring Festival and Mid-autumn Festival, while Chinese restaurants were heaved and bustled.

The reason? Cultural differences. Fast food restaurants like KFC and McDonald's are distinct American brands. Differences between China and US politics, economics, social development and ideology became obstacles to international enterprises operating in China. Corporate culture could not be understood or accepted here, especially in the restaurant field, where culture plays a crucial role.

McDonald's at full sail on the Huangpu River.

So the solution was to adapt: when in Rome, do as the Romans.

---

① whet [hwɛt] *vt.* 刺激
② jovial ['dʒoviəl] *adj.* 愉快的

贵的售价——10元一个汉堡,5元一杯可乐。

20世纪90年代中期,北京地区开了100家快餐店。方便、高效的服务,舒适的环境,悦耳的音乐和愉快的氛围吸引了大批粉丝。上班族喜欢在上班路上狼吞虎咽,朋友们喜欢喝杯可乐放松放松。尽管如此,目光敏锐的经理还是注意到有人过而不入。有的顾客抱怨快餐不如中餐好,而且品种单一。一到中国传统节日春节和中秋节,肯德基和麦当劳门可罗雀,而中餐厅则生意火爆。

这是为什么?文化差异。肯德基和麦当劳这种快餐厅是典型的美国牌子。中美政治、经济、社会发展和意识形态的差异成为跨国企业在中国运营的障碍。中国人不理解、也不接受西方的企业文化,尤其是深受文化影响的餐饮业。

麦当劳在黄浦江大获全胜

洋快餐的应对方法是:入乡随俗。中国饮食色香味俱全,种类繁多,快餐无法与之媲美,中国人的这种传统思想根深蒂固。人们的好奇心一旦消失,就会回头享受品种更加多样化的本土佳肴。在这种情况下,唯一的出路是结合两种不同的文化。快餐店一直在不断地学习和吸收中国文化的精髓。

2001年夏天以来,肯德基在菜单中增加了很多中国菜。四川榨菜和肉丝汤是首批菜肴。消费者在洋餐馆里品尝中国美食的同时,也感受到他们的传统正在受到尊重。这道汤成功之后,菜单上又很快增加了蘑菇米饭、番茄鸡蛋汤和老北京鸡肉卷。肯德基还推出含有牛肉、橙汁和新疆烧烤香料的快乐包薯条。

Deep-rooted in the Chinese consciousness is the traditional culture of food and drink that features color, fragrance, flavor and variety. Fast food simply does not compare. Now that curiosity had faded, people returned to their own more extensive cuisine. Under such circumstances, the only way out was to combine the two different cultures. Fast food restaurants have been learning to absorb elements of Chinese culture.

Since the summer of 2001, KFC has introduced many Chinese items onto their menus. Preserved Sichuan Pickle and Shredded Pork Soup was one of the first. Consumers felt their traditions were being respected when they could taste Chinese cuisine at a foreign restaurant. The soup proved a success, and Mushroom Rice, Tomato and Egg Soup, and Traditional Peking Chicken Roll were soon added to the menu. KFC also serves packets of Happy French Fry Shakes that contain beef, orange and Uygur barbecue spices.

Not content to lag behind, McDonald's Vegetable and Seafood Soup and Corn Soup were introduced, and the company worked to modify the restaurants' design. During the 2004 Spring Festival, McDonald's on Beijing's Wangfujing Street attracted many people with a traditional Chinese look, decorating their interiors with paper-cuts of the Chinese character Fu (Happiness), magpies① and twin fishes, all auspicious symbols.

Inter-cultural Management Mode

KFC and McDonald's have absorbed the Chinese cultural elements of showing respect, recognition, understanding, assimilation and amalgamation②, while maintaining the substance of the Western culture

---

① magpie ['mægpai] n. 喜鹊
② amalgamation [ə,mælgə'meiʃən] n. 混合

麦当劳不甘落后,推出了蔬菜海鲜汤和玉米汤,公司还花大气力修改了餐厅的设计。2004 年春节期间,麦当劳北京王府井店营造了一种传统的中国氛围,店内装饰了中国字"福"、喜鹊和双鱼等象征吉祥的剪纸,吸引了很多人。

文化交叉管理模式

为了表示对中国文化的尊重、认可、理解、同化和融合,肯德基和麦当劳在吸收中国文化诸多成分的同时,也保持了西方文化的实质,即效率、自由、民主、平等和人道。这种以美国商业文化为核心、以中国传统文化为补充的跨文化管理模式,为需要调整、充实和改造自身企业文化,以适应当地灵活的跨国企业市场提供了参考价值。

但是,实施跨文化管理模式也必须具备一定的条件。从客观上讲,为了使两种文化结合并同步发展,必须要有相似的环境。肯德基和麦当劳体现了人类与现代生活快节奏的和解,他们既是发展的产物,也是一种市场经济。他们共同产生的速度和效率仅对市场经济国家有意义。中国经济的发展速度为快餐文化提供了相应的环境和条件。快餐连锁店提供的服务表达了他们对自由和美国价值观的完美尊重,诠释了中国人思想包容的胸襟,他们渴望了解和体验西方的生活方式。两种文化主动碰撞、联结和同化。肯德基和麦当劳的本土化战略重新表达了美国的商业文化,他们使用中国传统文化的丰厚底蕴,在规范化管理的基础上,迎合了当地风俗。

of efficiency, freedom, democracy, equality and humanity. This inter-cultural management mode, with American business culture at the core, supplemented by Chinese traditional culture, provides reference for international enterprises which need to adjust, enrich and reconstruct their corporate culture to enhance local market flexibility.

There are, however, certain conditions essential to inter-cultural management mode. On the objective side, there must be similarities in environment in order for the two cultures to connect and synchronize. KFC and McDonald's embody an accommodation of the fast tempo of modern life: a product of development and a market economy. Their resultant speed and efficiency are only meaningful in countries with a market economy. China's rapid economic development offered the environmental conditions corresponding to fast food culture. Services offered by fast food chains express their full respect for freedom, an American value, as well as the psychological statement of Chinese open-mindedness that yearns to understand and experience the Western lifestyle. Two cultures proactively crashed, connected, and assimilated. KFC and McDonald's use the localization strategy to re-express American business culture, with profound traditional Chinese cultural emblems, catering to local customs on the basis of standardized management.

(845 words)

知识链接

America Tricon Global Restaurants　美国百胜全球餐饮集团。百胜餐饮集团是全球餐厅网络最大的餐饮集团，在全球 110 多个国家和地区拥有超过 35 000家连锁餐厅和 100 万多名员工。其旗下包括肯德基、必胜客、塔可钟、A&W 及 Long John Silver's（LJS），分别在烹鸡、比萨、墨西哥风味食品及海鲜连锁餐饮领域名列全球第一。

题　记

　　语言是一门艺术，是一组我们用于表达自己的思想和推己及人的文化信号。由于人们深受自己所处的社会和生活环境的影响，在交流中还是会出现一些障碍和问题。女性与成长于不同文化背景下的人们一样，通常都学过不同于男性的说话风格，这导致她们看起来没那么有竞争力和自信。音调、语速和停顿等语言的表达方式，不仅反映着人们的语言风格，也表达了谈话的技巧和威力。来自底特律的鲍勃与来自纽约的同事乔交谈时，很难插上嘴，因为他期待话轮转换之间的停顿比乔的实际停顿更长一些。同样，当萨利从德克萨斯搬到华盛顿特区后，却一直难以在员工会议上寻求插话的合理时间。虽然德克萨斯的人认为她乐于助人和充满自信，但华盛顿特区的人认为她腼腆害羞和不善社交。这种语言文化差异影响了我们对他人以及对他们能力的评价。

The Power of Talk

We all know what confidence, competence, and authority sound like. Or do we?

The head of a large division of a multinational corporation was running a meeting devoted to performance assessment. Each senior manager stood up, reviewed the individuals in his group, and evaluated them for promotion. Although there were women in every group, not one of them made the cut. One after another, each manager declared, in effect, that every woman in his group didn't have the self-confidence needed to be promoted. The division head began to doubt his ears. How could it be that all the talented women in the division suffered from a lack of self-confidence?

In all likelihood, they didn't. Consider the many women who have left large corporations to start their own businesses, obviously exhibiting enough confidence to succeed on their own. Judgments about confidence can be inferred only from the way people present themselves, and much of that presentation is in the form of talk.

The CEO of a major corporation told me that he often has to make

交谈的威力

我们似乎都知道什么是自信、能力和权威。 事实确实如此吗？

一家跨国公司的部门负责人正在主持绩效评估会议。 高级主管们逐个上台，回顾了团队成员的业绩，并对他们的晋升做出评价。 尽管每个团队都有女性，她们中却没有一个人获得晋升的机会。 主管们相继表示，实际上，他们团队里的所有女性都缺乏晋升所必需的自信。 这位部门负责人开始怀疑他的耳朵：本部门所有能干的女性都缺乏自信，这怎么可能呢？

她们十有八九并非如此。 想想众多的离开大公司自己创业的女人，她们显然表现出了成功应有的自信。 判断自信只能通过观察人们自身的表现，尤其是交谈的表现。

一位大公司的总裁告诉我，他常常只用 5 分钟对别人可能花 5 个月处理的事情做决定。 他介绍了他使用的准则：如果制订计划的人显得信心十足，总裁就会通过，不然就否决。 这个方法看似合情合理，但我的研究领域显示，社会语言学并不赞同这种观点。 总裁显然认为自己知道什么样的人拥有自信，但他的判断对有些人来说完全正确，而对其他人则是完全错误的。

decisions in five minutes about matters on which others may have worked five months. He said he uses this rule: If the person making the proposal seems confident, the CEO approves it. If not, he says no. This might seem like a reasonable approach. But my field of research, socio-linguistics, suggests otherwise. The CEO obviously thinks he knows what a confident person sounds like. But his judgment, which may be dead right for some people, may be dead wrong for others.

Communication isn't as simple as saying what you mean. How you say what you mean is crucial, and differs from one person to the next, because using language is learned social behavior: How we talk and listen are deeply influenced by cultural experience. Although we might think that our ways of saying what we mean are natural, we can run into trouble if we interpret and evaluate others as if they necessarily felt the same way we'd feel if we spoke the way they did.

For many years, I have been researching the influence of linguistic style on conversations and human relationships. In the past several years, I have extended that research to the workplace, where I have observed how ways of speaking learned in childhood affect judgments of competence and confidence, as well as who gets heard, who gets credit, and what gets done.

The division head who was dumbfounded① to hear that all the talented women in his organization lacked confidence was probably right

---

① dumbfound [dʌm'faund] *vt.* 使发愣

188

交流不是简单地说清楚你的意思。 如何表达你的意思、并讲得与众不同起着决定性的作用，因为语言的使用是习得的社会行为：我们如何交谈和如何倾听都深受文化经历的影响。 尽管我们也许认为自己表达意思的方式很正常，但如果我们讲话的方式与他们一样，他们可能必然地与我们有同样的感受，假如按这种方式理解和评价他人，我们就会陷入困境。

多年来，我一直在研究语言风格对交谈和人际关系的影响。 在过去的几年中，我把这类研究扩展到工作场所，我在那里观察了儿童期语言学习的方式，以及这种方式如何影响对能力和自信做出判断，包括谁听到了他们的声音，谁取得了他们的信任，他们又做了些什么。

听说公司里所有能干的女性都缺乏自信，那位部门主管难免目瞪口呆，这种质疑的态度或许是正确的。 高管们按照自己的语言规范来评价团队中的女性，但是女性与成长于不同文化背景下的人们一样，通常都学过不同于男性的说话风格，这导致她们看起来没那么有竞争力和自信。

什么是语言风格？

不管说什么都必须按某种方式表达：一种特定的语调、一种特定的语速和一种特定程度的声调。 尽管我们在说话前经常有意识地思考要说什么，但是我们很少考虑如何去说，除非是在有明显准备的情况下，例如求职面试或棘手的业绩审查。 语言风格指人们特定的说话模式。 它包括直接或间接、语速和停顿、词语选择，以及对

to be skeptical. The senior managers were judging the women in their groups by their own linguistic norms, but women — like people who have grown up in a different culture — have often learned different styles of speaking than men, which can make them seem less competent and self-assured than they are.

What Is Linguistic Style?

Everything that is said must be said in a certain way — in a certain tone of voice, at a certain rate of speed, and with a certain degree of loudness. Whereas often we consciously consider what to say before speaking, we rarely think about how to say it, unless the situation is obviously loaded — for example, a job interview or a tricky performance review. Linguistic style refers to a person's characteristic speaking pattern. It includes such features as directness or indirectness, pacing and pausing, word choice, and the use of such elements as jokes, figures of speech, stories, questions, and apologies. In other words, linguistic style is a set of culturally learned signals by which we not only communicate what we mean but also interpret others' meaning and evaluate one another as people.

Consider turn taking, one element of linguistic style. Conversation is an enterprise in which people take turns: One person speaks, and then the other responds. However, this apparently simple exchange requires a subtle negotiation of signals so that you know when the other person is finished and it's your turn to begin. Cultural factors such as country or region of origin and ethnic background influence how long a pause seems

笑话、名言、故事、问题、道歉等元素的使用。 换句话说，语言风格是一组文化学术信号，我们不仅用它来表达自己的意思，而且用它来解释他人的意思，并像普通人一样用它来相互评估。

再考虑语言风格中的另一个元素——话轮转换。 会话是一项集体的活动，人们轮流发言，即一个人说，然后其他人做出回应。 但是，这种简单明了的互换需要一个细微的协商信号，这样你才知道其他人什么时候结束发言，你什么时候开始讲话。 多长时间的停顿才显得自然，似乎取决于国籍、出生地和种族背景等文化因素的影响。 来自底特律的鲍勃与来自纽约的同事乔交谈时，很难插上嘴，因为他期待话轮转换之间的停顿比乔的实际停顿更长一些。 而那种长度的停顿却从未出现，因为在它还没发生以前，乔就感觉到了不舒适的沉默，然后这段时间他自己就讲得更多。 两个人都没有意识到，话语风格差异阻碍了他们的交流。 鲍勃认为乔爱出风头，而且对自己要说的事情毫无兴趣，而乔却认为鲍勃没什么可说的。 同样，当萨利从得克萨斯搬到华盛顿特区后，她一直在员工会议上寻求插话的合理时间，却一直没能如愿以偿。 虽然德克萨斯的人认为她乐于助人和充满自信，但华盛顿特区的人认为她腼腆害羞和不善社交。 她的老板甚至建议她参加自信心培训课程。 所以，话语风格的细微差异可以对听到声音的人和正在做判断的人产生令人惊讶的影响，包括心理上的影响。 在这些例子中，哪怕是几秒钟的停顿也会产生不同的效果，这些差异影响了我们对他人以及对他们能力的评价。

natural. When Bob, who is from Detroit, has a conversation with his colleague Joe, from New York City, it's hard for him to get a word in edgewise① because he expects a slightly longer pause between turns than Joe does. A pause of that length never comes because, before it has a chance to, Joe senses an uncomfortable silence, which he fills with more talk of his own. Both men fail to realize that differences in conversational style are getting in their way. Bob thinks that Joe is pushy and uninterested in what he has to say, and Joe thinks that Bob doesn't have much to contribute. Similarly, when Sally relocated from Texas to Washington, D. C., she kept searching for the right time to break in during staff meetings — and never found it. Although in Texas she was considered outgoing and confident, in Washington she was perceived as shy and retiring. Her boss even suggested she take an assertiveness② training course. Thus slight differences in conversational style — in these cases, a few seconds of pause — can have a surprising impact on who gets heard and on the judgments, including psychological ones, that are made about people and their abilities.

(875 words)

---

① edgewise ['edʒwaiz] *adv.* 从旁边
② assertive [ə'sɜːtiv] *adj.* 表现自信的

知识链接

Linguistic Style　　语言风格是人们运用语言表达手段形成的诸特点的综合表现，它包括语言的民族风格、时代风格、流派风格、个人风格、语体风格和表现风格，并在主客观因素制导下运用语言表达手段的诸特点综合表现出来的格调与气氛。现代语言风格学包括三方面：词汇风格、句法风格和韵律风格。

题　记

　　在宣传低碳经济的今天，远程办公具有无可比拟的优越性。那些最先领悟到这一点的公司，可以拥有最好的竞争力——更低的办公室租金、更加身心健康的员工、更加积极向上的气氛、尤其是更低的离职率。当然，远程办公的顺利实施需要公司和个人必要的设备支持，公司还要在远程办公的管理模式上作一些细节的考虑。作为远程办公的受益者之一，员工们可以实现自由选择办公环境的梦想——可以是家里，可以是咖啡店，可以是某个农村的小院子，并且随时随地和家人在一起。随着宽带网和虚拟专用网的出现，越来越多的企业开始考虑远程家庭办公这种工作方式。

Making Telecommuting Work

'Teleworking' can lower overhead, raise productivity, and make employees happy. Kathy Durfee, founder and CEO of nine-person TechHouse, a Bradenton Fla. consulting company, admits that her management style was shaped by stints at big companies such as PepsiCo and Accenture. "I had it in my mind that an office should be very structured, " she says. That meant no jeans in the office, fixed work schedules, and no telecommuting. Several years ago, when several of her employees asked if they could work from home occasionally, Durfee said no. "I didn't think we could function, " she says. "I was worried things would be dropped."

Once, a star employee went out on short-term disability. The only way he could stay with TechHouse was to work from home part-time. The arrangement was a bust①, and he left. "The fact it didn't work with him set off alarm bells, " Durfee says. "I don't want to be in a position where I can't keep a good employee." Durfee realized she needed to make

---

① bust [bʌst] *n.* 破产

远 程 办 公

"远程办公"可以节省日常开支、提高效率以及让员工快乐。位于佛罗里达州布雷登顿的九人科技咨询公司的创始人及首席执行官凯茜·德菲承认，她在效力百事和埃森哲等大公司时形成了自己的管理风格。 她声称："我曾一度认为办公室应该中规中矩。"也就是说，在办公室不能穿牛仔裤，按固定的工作时间表上班，没有远程办公。 几年前，当她的几个员工询问是否可以偶尔在家办公时，凯茜一口回绝了他们。 她说："我认为这样做行不通。 我担心会误事。"

一次，一位明星员工要暂时离开公司休伤残假。 他要继续留在科技咨询公司的唯一办法是在家做兼职。 因为这个计划落了空，所以他被迫离开公司。 德菲表示："他的离开给我敲响了警钟。 我不希望自己留不住好员工。"德菲意识到，她必须实行远程办公的模式。 此后，她分别在奥兰多和克利尔沃特聘请了两名咨询顾问。她在布雷登顿雇用了三名远程办公的员工，其中包括技术总监。 德菲现在认为，她当初因远程办公而误开了那名员工在某种程度上是由于缺乏沟通，所以她定期召开办公会议，强制执行相关条款，要

telecommuting work. She has since hired two consultants who work from Orlando and Clearwater. Three of the Bradenton staff telecommute, including the chief technology officer. Durfee now thinks her early misfire with telecommuting was due in part to poor communication, so she holds mandatory① office meetings and enforces protocols about when employees should use telephone, e-mail, or instant messaging to contact one another.

Telecommuting, or "teleworking" in consultant-speak, is growing among small businesses. "We are seeing more small companies than ever before embrace this," says Mike Williams, director of programs and employer services at the Atlanta-based nonprofit Clean Air Campaign, which helps companies set up telecommuting programs. The number of people working away from the office at least once a month has been growing at about 10% annually for several years, hitting 35 million this year, according to WorldatWork, an association for human resource professionals. About 12% of employees at companies with 21 to 100 people sometimes work remotely, according to a survey by technology company CDW.

The company's policy should state which jobs can be done remotely and how often. Jobs that don't require face time, or that involve longer periods of concentration, are good candidates. Even managers may have duties, such as writing reports, that ideally are completed in splendid

---

① mandatory ['mændətəri] *adj.* 强制性的

求员工使用电话、电子邮件或实时通讯互相联系。

商务咨询交谈中的远程办公或"电子办公"在小型企业之间与日俱增。 位于亚特兰大的非盈利性清洁空气运动项目和雇主服务主管迈克·威廉姆斯说："我们发现实行远程办公的小企业比以往更多了。"这种模式帮助公司建立了远程办公的程序。 根据人力资源专家协会 WorldatWork 的统计，每月至少一次不在办公室办公的人数连续几年按每年 10% 的速度增长，今年更是达到了 3 500 万人的高峰。计算机中心公司下属的科技公司的一份调查显示，在规模为 21 人至 100 人的公司中，大约 12% 的雇员有时远程办公。

公司的政策应该阐明，哪些工作可以远程完成，以及多长时间一次完成一项任务。 那些不需要会面时间或者需要较长时间关注的工作很适合远程办公。 经理们也要承担写报告之类的职责，有些任务最好是在完全隔离的状态下完成。

哪些人适合远程办公不能仅凭工作类型决定，那些需要大量指导和激励的人就不是合适的人选。 员工在独立工作之前，应该在办公室花足够的时间掌握工作技巧。 为了消除那些需要待在办公室的员工的抱怨情绪，公司可以提供公交补贴等福利。 另外，公司也应讲清楚需要什么样的远程办公人员以及谁来支付远程办公设备的费用。

很多公司为雇员配备笔记本电脑，便于他们在家庭与公司之间奔波时随身携带。 远程工作者为工作提供了一个独立的空间，避免了上班时间因为惦记孩子而出现的工作分心。 如果有人一个星期里

isolation.

It's not just the job that determines who can telecommute. Someone who needs lots of direction or prodding may not be a good candidate. And employees should spend enough time in the office to learn the ropes before they're on their own. To head off resentment among those who need to stay on site, you might offer a benefit such as a subsidy for public transportation. You should also spell out what sort of home office employees need and who will pay for the requisite technology.

Most businesses outfit employees with a laptop they can schlep between home and work. The telecommuter provides a separate space for work and avoids distractions — such as child care — while on the clock. If someone is working four or more days a week from home, most companies pick up the cost of Internet access, a phone line, and, if necessary, equipment for teleconferencing.

The company may also want to rethink guidelines for productivity. For customer service jobs, it might be relatively straightforward: How many complaints got resolved that day? For others, some managers may want an e-mail outlining what the staffer will do each day. Then there's Durfee's approach: "A great employee wants to work," she says. "And if someone doesn't want to work, they can avoid working in the office, too." The important thing is to lay out how expectations will be set and communicated. Remember that some people work better in an office environment and should stay there. So don't pressure people to telecommute. "Not everybody wants to do this," says Gil Gordon, a

有 4 天或是更多的时间在家工作，大部分企业会承担上网费、电话费，如果必要的话，还会提供电话会议所需的设备。

如果企业考虑到工作效率，可能会重新审视这些指导方针。 对于客服工作来说，这样做可能相对直截了当：一天内解决了多少投诉？ 而对于其他的工作来说，有些经理可能会要求一封电子邮件，罗列出工作人员每天的工作计划。 而德菲的态度是："优秀的员工希望工作，如果有人不想工作，他们也可以避免在办公室工作。"关键是要确定预期目标和沟通方式。 请记住，要让那些在办公室里工作做得更出色的人待在办公室里，不要强迫他们远程工作。 吉尔·戈登是一名咨询顾问，他公司的总部设在新泽西州蒙默思郡的交叉路口。 他认为"并不是每个人都喜欢远程工作，有些人不想把工作带回家"。

布莱斯的两名员工正在远程办公，一名是账户经理，另一名是呼叫中心代理。 布莱斯希望其他员工也可以尽快开始远程办公。布莱斯说："我只收到了积极的反馈。"即便公司的员工已经增加到19 人，但是布莱斯只需要为 15 名员工提供办公桌，所以每月可以节省 500 美元的租金。

当然，科技手段和雇员们不能总在第一次就将工作完成得尽善尽美。 对总部位于亚特兰大的商业室内设计公司 VeenendaalCave 的总裁爱德华·凯乌来说，试行已就绪。 在资产达 700 万美元的公司里，62 名员工需要经常合作，他的设计师们非常依赖公司的书库和材料样品。 凯乌表示，"一想到员工们身穿睡衣，边工作边看奥普

consultant based in Monmouth Junction, N.J. "Some people don't want their work to come home with them."

Two of Blythe's employees are telecommuting: an account manager and a call center agent. Blythe expects others will start soon. "I've had nothing but positive feedback," Blythe says. He plans to provide desks for only 15 people even as his company grows to 19 employees, saving about $ 500 a month in rent.

Of course, neither technology nor employees always perform perfectly the first time out. For Edward A. Cave, president of Atlanta-based commercial interior design firm VeenendaalCave, a trial run was in order. The 62 employees of his $ 7 million company need to collaborate frequently, and his designers rely heavily on the company's library of books and materials samples. "It's scary for an employer," says Cave. "You have images of people working in their pajamas watching Oprah."

Cave and partner Christine Veenendaal decided to allow employees six telework days a year. Only the receptionist and two IT managers are ineligible. Would-be telecommuters must notify a manager 48 hours in advance that they plan to work from home, to make sure they've thought about which materials they need to have with them. Employees must have high-speed Internet access at home, a landline phone, and a home computer and printer. Modest as the program is, Cave says it's been a big hit, and he's considering expanding it.

As the real estate market was collapsing, Communiqué Group CEO Micki Clark reluctantly shut the Denver office of her resort real estate

拉的节目，老板就会提心吊胆"。

凯乌和他的合伙人克里斯廷·威尼达尔决定允许员工们每年中有 6 天时间进行远程办公。 只有接待员和两个系统管理员没有资格。 想要成为远程办公者必须提前 48 小时通知经理，以确保经理们可以考虑远程办公需要哪些材料。 员工的家中要能高速联网，有一部座机，一台家用电脑和一台打印机。 凯乌表示，尽管这个项目不大，但它已经产生了巨大的影响，他正在考虑扩大这个项目。

由于房地产市场正在崩溃，联合公告集团的首席执行官米奇·克拉克很不情愿地关闭了她的度假房地产营销公司在丹佛的办公室，并要求 9 位美国雇员远程办公。 她说也在公司上班的女儿杰西卡听了这个想法后拉着她"又喊又叫"。 克拉克说："我是大老板。我已经从事这个职业 20 年了，并且我喜欢密切注视别人"。 但是，现在价值 430 万美元的公司正在节省每月 1.6 万美元的租金。 随着产业的彻底失败，克拉克声称："我们这样做是为了将来的生活而再战"。

米奇每周一在本地的潘娜拉餐厅召开员工会议。 员工们把他们本周的工作计划交给杰西卡，并请求帮助。 那些经常在一起工作的人通常聚集在附近有无线网络的建筑物中。 现在，克拉克的生活已经发生了改变，在本该走在早晨的上班路上的时候，她却骑着马在自家 40 英亩的牧场里溜达。 她表示："没有人想重返办公室了。"当然也包括她自己。

marketing firm, asking the nine U.S. employees to telecommute. She says her daughter Jessica, who also works in the business, had to drag her "kicking and screaming" to the idea. "I'm an old broad, " Clark says. "I've done this for 20 years and I like to keep an eye on people." But now the $ 4.3 million company is saving about $ 16,000 a month in rent. With her industry in meltdown, "We are doing this to live to fight another day, " says Clark.

Micki holds staff meetings every Monday at a local Panera restaurant. Employees give Jessica their to-do lists for the week and ask for any help they need. Those who are working together often retreat to a nearby atrium that has wireless Internet access. Now Clark, who rides horses at her 40-acre ranch during what used to be her morning commute, is a convert. "Nobody wants to go back to an office, " she says. Including her.

(1,078 words)

知识链接 🔍

WorldatWork 美国人力资源调研集团 WorldatWork 是世界上致力于薪酬、福利和全面报酬方面领先知识的顶级协会，成立于 1955 年，专注于吸引、保留和激励员工相关的人力资源科学，是薪酬专业资格认证(CCP)、福利专业资格认证(CBPTM)、全球薪酬管理师认证(GRP)、国际人力资源管理专业资格认证 (IMHR)的认证机构，其会员中有25 000名都是影响、开发和执行员工报酬体系的专家，100%受雇于财富1 000强企业，99%受雇于财富500强企业。

题　记

　　自由贸易和保护贸易这对矛盾运动，在国与国之间的博弈中谨慎发展，在全球经济一体化的背景下蹒跚前行。巴拉克·奥巴马和希拉里·克林顿作为倡议者签署了一份新法案：如果人民币不升值，就要对其提高关税。他们的立场反映了一个广为接受的观点：和发展中国家进行自由贸易是美国富人们的伎俩，他们从中牟利，而美国平民却承担成本。事实上，在自由贸易中遭受损失最惨重的那些人常常是自由贸易的最大受益者。美国穷人在"非耐用品"上的消费比富人要多40%。这就意味着在与发展中国家的贸易中，美国低收入者从低廉的价格中得到了大得多的好处。贸易壁垒本身就是一把双刃剑，自由贸易使普通美国人暗中窃喜——他们的钱正在原本的价值上不断增值……

The Free-Trade Paradox

All the acrimony① in the primary race between Barack Obama and Hillary Clinton has disguised the fact that on most issues they're not too far apart. That's especially the case when it comes to free trade, which both Obama and Clinton have lambasted② over the past few months. At times, the campaign has looked like a contest over who hates free trade more: Obama has argued that free-trade agreements like NAFTA are bought and paid for by special interests, while Clinton has emphasized the need to "stand up" to certain countries. Two weeks ago, both senators signed on as sponsors of a new bill that would effectively impose higher tariffs on RMB if it doesn't revalue its currency. The candidates are trying to win the favor of unions and blue-collar voters in states like Ohio and West Virginia, of course, but their positions also reflect a widespread belief that free trade with developing countries is a kind of scam perpetrated③ by the wealthy, who reap the benefits while ordinary Americans bear the cost.

---

① acrimony [ˈækriməni] n. 言谈举止上的讽刺
② lambaste [læmˈbeist] vi. 严责
③ perpetrate [ˈpəːpitreit] vt. 作恶

自由贸易悖论

　　巴拉克·奥巴马和希拉里·克林顿在初选中针锋相对，不过，双方都掩盖了这样一个事实：在大多数议题上他们不会有太大分歧。 尤其是在过去的几个月里，他们一直在抨击的自由贸易。 有时候，选举运动就像是在比谁更讨厌自由贸易一样。 奥巴马认为，购买和支付《北美自由贸易协定》中规定的自由贸易商品是出于某些特殊利益的考虑，而希拉里则强调需要"抵制"某些国家。 两个星期以前，这两位参议员作为倡议者都签署了一份新法案：如果人民币不升值，就要对其提高关税。 这两位候选人都希望通过这项法案获得俄亥俄州和西弗吉尼亚州工会和蓝领工人的支持。 当然，他们的立场也反映了一个广为接受的观点：和发展中国家进行自由贸易是美国富人们的伎俩，他们从中牟利，而美国平民却承担成本。

　　这是一个很容易让人接受的观点：毕竟美国工人和那些每小时报酬才 70 美分的其他国家的工人相比怎么会有竞争优势呢？ 事实上，自由贸易对美国人工资的负面影响并不是这么容易定论的。 例如，虽然经济学家保罗·克鲁格曼在最近的学术论文中推断，对这些影响不可能进行量化分析，但他认为影响是显著的。 可以很肯定地说，自由贸易带来的失业和工资下降的压力主要落在美国中产阶

209

It's an understandable view: how, after all, can it be a good thing for American workers to have to compete with people who get paid seventy cents an hour? As it happens, the negative effect of trade on American wages isn't that easy to document. The economist Paul Krugman, for instance, believes that the effect is significant, though in a recent academic paper he concluded that it was impossible to quantify. But it's safe to say that the main burden of trade-related job losses and wage declines has fallen on middle- and lower-income Americans. So standing up to China seems like a logical way to help ordinary Americans do better. But there's a problem with this approach: the very people who suffer most from free trade are often, paradoxically, among its biggest beneficiaries.

The reason for this is simple: free trade with poorer countries has a huge positive impact on the buying power of middle- and lower-income consumers — a much bigger impact than it does on the buying power of wealthier consumers. The less you make, the bigger the percentage of your spending that goes to manufactured goods — clothes, shoes, and the like — whose prices are often directly affected by free trade. The wealthier you are, the more you tend to spend on services — education, leisure, and so on — that are less subject to competition from abroad. In a recent paper on the effect of trade with the developing countries, the University of Chicago economists Christian Broda and John Romalis estimate that poor Americans devote around forty per cent more of their spending to "non-durable goods" than rich Americans do. That means that lower-income Americans get a much bigger benefit from the lower

210

级和低收入者的身上。 因此，为了改善美国平民的境况，强势反对
中国似乎是一个合理的方法。 但是，这么做有个问题：在自由贸易
中遭受损失最惨重的那些人常常是自由贸易的最大受益者，这真是
自相矛盾。

这样做的理由很简单：与较贫困的国家进行自由贸易对中产阶
级和低收入者的购买力有着巨大的积极影响，而这远远大于对富人
购买力的影响。 你赚的钱越少，花费在日常用品上的开支占总支出
的比例就会越大，如衣服、鞋子等商品的价格常常直接受自由贸易
的牵制。 你越富有，花在教育、休闲等其他服务上的消费就会越
多，来自国外的竞争较少涉及这些领域。 芝加哥大学的经济学家克
里斯蒂安·布罗达和约翰·罗马里斯最近发表了一篇文章，研究与
发展中国家贸易带来的影响。 他们在论文中指出，美国穷人在"非
耐用品"上的消费比富人要多 40%。 这就意味着在与发展中国家的
贸易中，美国低收入者从低廉的价格中得到了大得多的好处。

另外，与美国富人购买的产品相比，美国中产阶级和低收入者
更可能购买原产地在发展中国家的商品。 尽管来自发展中国家的进
口已经大大增加，占美国进口总比例的六分之一，但这些产品仍然
大多集中在低价市场。 据有关方面的估计，沃尔玛最近几年从发展
中国家的进口约占总进口的十分之一。 与之形成对照的是，较富裕
的美国人购买的商品大部分是美国制造，或是德国和瑞士等高工资
国家制造。 路易威登箱包、百达翡丽手表等奢侈品广受富人的欢
迎，电子产品、厨房用具、家具以及欧美制造商生产的许多其他商
品同样占据着高端市场，销售持续火爆。 耶鲁大学的经济学家彼
得·司各特认为，发达国家制造的机械和电子产品在美国的卖价是

prices that trade with the developing countries has brought.

Then, too, the specific products that middle- and lower-income Americans buy are much more likely to originate in developing countries than the products that wealthier Americans buy. Despite a huge increase in imports from developing countries — they sextupled① as a percentage of U. S. imports between — those products are still concentrated mostly in lower-price markets. By some estimates, Wal-Mart alone has accounted for nearly a tenth of all imports from developing countries in recent years. By contrast, much of what wealthier Americans buy is made in the U.S. or in high-wage countries like Germany and Switzerland. This is obvious when it comes to luxury goods — Louis Vuitton bags, Patek Philippe watches, and so on — but it's also true of many other goods, like electronics, kitchen appliances, and furniture, categories in which American and European manufacturers have continued to thrive by selling to the high-end market. According to the Yale economist Peter K. Schott, machinery and electronics products made in developed countries sell in the U.S. for four times the average price of the products of the developing countries. And, since the late nineteen-eighties, that price gap has widened by almost forty per cent.

This may not always be the case. For example, as China's economy continues to boom, its companies will likely move up the quality ladder and, eventually, become serious competition for high-end American and European manufacturers. But for the moment the benefits of free trade

---

① sextuple ['sekstjupl] *vi.* 变成六倍

发展中国家制造的产品的平均价格的四倍。 并且，自 20 世纪 80 年代末以来，这个价格差距已经扩大了 40% 。

　　情况可能也并非总是如此。 例如，随着中国经济的持续繁荣，中国的公司很可能提高产品的质量，最终与欧美制造商争夺高端市场。 但是绝大多数的美国普通民众目前正在集中享受与中国自由贸易的好处，至少是购物的好处。 结果，在过去的 10 年中，与富人的购物开销相比，他们购买的产品要便宜得多。 根据布罗达和罗马里斯在近期论文中的统计，仅在过去的 3 年间，美国低收入者的通货膨胀率差不多比美国最富的那些人的通货膨胀率低 7 个百分点。这也表明，与中国的自由贸易给美国平民、至少是消费者带来了更多的好处。 从这个意义上讲，自由贸易使美国人的钱比原本的价值更值钱。

　　现在，许多残留的因素都在试图打破这个平衡，例如，自由贸易可能通过增加公司的利润而使美国的富人更富有。 总而言之，廉价的 DVD 不可能补偿失业的痛苦。 但现实是，如果我们加强与发展中国家的贸易关系，也只有少数人获利，因为在那些直接与发展中国家的制造商竞争的公司上班的人员毕竟有限，而普通美国人面对更高的价格只会感到痛苦，将会比美国富人更快、更直接地感受到痛苦。 奥巴马和希拉里的本意是帮助美国的工薪阶层，并且得到他们的选票，但他们推行的这些政策也会伤害他们。

知识链接 🔍

NAFTA 北美自由贸易协定（North American Free Trade Agreement）。由美

with China, at least when it comes to shopping, are concentrated overwhelmingly among average Americans. And the result is that, in the past decade, the products that they spend more on have become a lot cheaper compared to the stuff that rich people spend more on. Broda and Romalis, in their recent paper, calculate that in the past three years alone the inflation rate for lower-income Americans was almost seven points lower than it was for the wealthiest Americans. That means that free trade with China has made average Americans, at least as consumers, much better off — in the sense that it's made their dollars go further than they otherwise would have.

Now, there's a lot that's left out of this equation, such as the fact that free trade may help richer Americans by increasing corporate profits. And cheap DVD players may not, on balance, make up for lost jobs. But the reality is that if we toughen our trade relations with the developing countries the benefits will be enjoyed by a few, since only a small percentage of Americans now work for companies that compete directly with the manufacturers in developing countries, while average Americans will feel the pain — in the form of higher prices — far more quickly and more directly than rich Americans will. Obama and Clinton, in their desire to help working Americans — and gain their votes — are pushing for policies that will also hurt them.

(940 words)

国、加拿大和墨西哥三方于 1992 年签订、1994 年元旦起生效和实施。内容有：①关税相互减免；②取消进口限制；③坚持产地规定；④政府采购协定；⑤鼓励投资；⑥扩大相互金融服务；⑦发展相互自由运输；⑧鼓励保护知识产权；⑨协商争端解决机制等。1994 年，国会通过了北美自由贸易协定，美国前总统比尔·克林顿将其写入法律。今天，这 3 个北美自由贸易协定成员国已经有 417 万的共同人口和超过 11 万亿美元的国内生产总值。

题　记

曾几何时，家族企业依靠血缘关系所产生的强大凝聚力，以其灵活的经营管理机制，能够及时抓住市场机遇，使企业在短时间内得以迅速成长壮大。无论经营与管理，美国家族企业都比那些谈不上血脉相继的竞争对手更胜一筹，其延续千年的秘诀就是发现并保存了企业的核心价值，为吸引顾客和家族后代持续经营提供了长久的支持。经久不衰的家族企业始于持之以恒的目标，培养代代传承的企业激情，在此基础上建立强大的法律框架，并运用良好的沟通构筑横贯家族企业基础中的水泥钢筋。在历经沧桑、浪淘尽千古风流的历史长河中，每一个拥有百年历史的公司都建立了坚如磐石的职业道德，保证企业在经济体制剧烈变革、游戏规则不断变更的背景下走向成熟。

Building a Family
Business to Last

Forget for a moment the dismal① statistics about family business survival. Consider the hundreds of family businesses that have persevered, not just for a generation, but for centuries. You may not be in a position to challenge what may be the world's oldest continuously operating family business, Japanese hotel Ryokan Hoshi, which was founded in 717 and today is run by the 46th generation of the Hoshi family. But such extreme cases do prove that family businesses — possibly including yours — can last a very long time.

If you want your family business to endure, strengthen it from the foundation up. Making a conscious choice to create a long-lived company is the first step in building a strong foundation. It takes some luck to survive for generations, certainly, but these things don't happen by accident either. It starts with your intentions.

Realize that seeking a long life isn't the only valid choice. Some businesses are appropriately designed for short life. Depending on the opportunity that presents itself, it may be best for all concerned if you

① dismal ['dizml] *adj.* 令人沮丧的

建立持久的家族企业

暂时别管那些令人沮丧的关于家族企业生存状况的统计数据。想一想数以百计的家族企业，他们代代相传，世纪连绵。 世界上持续经营最久的家族企业——日本的法师旅馆，成立于717年，目前的老板是第46代传人。 你也许没有能力挑战法师旅馆，但是这种极端的例子的确证明了家族企业可以持续很长一段时间，也可能包括你的家族企业。

如果你希望自己的家族企业经久不衰，就必须从打基础开始持之以恒。 选择有意识地创造一个长寿的公司，这是建立坚实基础的第一步。 当然，代代相传还需要一些运气，但这些事情也不会从天而降。 建立持久的家族企业始于你的目标。

要意识到，建立持久的家族企业并不是唯一有效的选择。 有些企业适合短期经营。 根据眼前的机遇，如果建立一个起步快、增长迅速的公司，然后将它出售或与另一家公司合并，这对相关各方也许是最好的选择。 扪心自问，你是否真的希望自己承担责任，实现公司长久和独立生存的目标。

一旦做出决定，建立激情应该是下一个目标。 你也许拥有满腔热情，但很可能瞬间烟消云散。 必须有人把这种激情传给年轻的一

design a company that will start fast, grow quickly, and then be sold or merged with another. Ask yourself whether you truly want to commit yourself and your company to the goal of a long and independent life.

Once you've made the decision, building passion should be your next objective. You may have all the passion you need, but you won't be around forever. Someone must engender① passion in younger generations. Start by exposing children to your business. Take them to work with you. Tell them about the things that you love in your business. Mentor② them to have a romance with the enterprise. Then, make sure they have the training and experience needed to give that passion balance. Encourage and enable them to get appropriate university degrees. Enforce a requirement that future family business leaders get work experience in other companies before taking jobs in the family enterprise. Broad and deep preparation, both mental and emotional, is required of leaders of long-lived family businesses.

At the same time, make sure your business has good governance in place. This means creating a board with a significant number of outside directors. It means building long-term relationships with nonfamily advisers who are both expert and independent, and won't just tell you what you want to hear. It means having policies that create accountability③. In practical terms, if a family member executive or director isn't acting in the company's best interests, you need a way for the board to replace him or her. Otherwise, you don't have true

---

① engender [in'dʒendə] *vt.* 产生,引起
② mentor ['mɛn'tɔr] *vt.* 引导,指导
③ accountability [əkauntə'biliti] *n.* 有责任

代。 首先，让孩子们接触你的企业。 带他们和你一起工作。 告诉他们你喜欢的一些业务。 引导他们对企业产生一种浪漫情怀。 然后，务必让他们参加培训，获得经验，以保持激情的平衡。 对他们加以鼓励，并使他们能够获得适当的大学学位。 强行要求未来的家族企业领袖到其他企业获得相关的工作经验，然后再接手家族企业。 历时长久的家族企业领袖需要从精神上和情绪上做好广泛而深入的准备。

与此同时，务必使你的企业治理得当。 这就是说，要建立一个包括大量外部董事的董事会。 这意味着与非家族成员建立长期的合作关系，外部董事既专业又独立，他们不会只拣你喜欢的说。 这也意味着企业可以采用问责制的管理模式。 实际上，如果担任总裁或主管的某个家庭成员没有按照公司的最大利益原则从事，你需要有办法把他或她踢出董事会。 否则，公司没有真正的问责制，公司的未来也可能受到限制。

历久弥新的家族企业也源于拥有一个强大的规则框架。 股东协议和补偿政策之类的文件也许看上去只是法律文书，但是它们在家族企业遇到继承、冲突或其他压力等灭顶之灾时，实际上是治疗混乱和争议的良药。 忽视遗嘱、买卖协议或股利支付政策似乎都会给家族企业带来麻烦。 要保持公司的健康发展，婚前协议、就业政策以及其他你期望界定强大、持久商业结构的公司文件就十分重要。

沟通是家族企业的基石中横贯水泥的钢筋。 如果你不能有效表达承诺、激情、问责制和引领企业的规则，怎么能指望他人对你的认同呢？ 如果你不能理解他人在多大程度上认同你的承诺和其他方面，那么你就是盲目经营，肯定会惹上麻烦。

accountability, and your company's future may be constrained.

Longevity also springs from having a robust legal framework. They may seem like mere paperwork, but documents such as shareholders' agreements and compensation policies are actually vaccinations against the viruses of confusion and contention that can eat up family businesses experiencing succession, conflict, or other stress. Neglecting wills, buy-sell agreements, or dividend payout policies is akin to inviting disease into your home. Keep your company healthy with prenuptial agreements, employment policies, and other corporate documents defining the strong and lasting business structure that you desire.

Communication is the rebar that runs through the cement in this foundation. If you don't effectively express the commitment, passion, accountability, and rules guiding your business, how can you expect others to buy in? And if you don't understand the extent to which others have accepted your commitment and the rest as their own, then you are building blind and headed for trouble. Excellent communication begins not with speaking, but with listening. By carefully and consciously hearing the thoughts and feelings of the people you want to influence, you gain the knowledge you must have to cast your expressions so that they are understood. Echoing or restating the statements of others is a good basic tool for reassuring them that you are listening, as well as alerting both of you to potential miscommunications or misunderstandings.

After you have listened and understood what you are up against, you are ready to express yourself. Everyone has heard that the three vital attributes of real estate are location, location, and location. Similarly, a great writer once said that three things are most important in communication: clarity, clarity, and clarity. If you strive for nothing else

良好的沟通始于倾听而非侃侃而谈。 仔细并有意识地听取目标对象的想法和感受，你才能获得与之沟通的必要信息，进而使你的理念有效地影响他。 回应和重述他人的观点是一个不错的基本沟通技巧，它能够使别人确信你正在倾听，也可以消除你们之间可能产生的沟通不畅和误解。

听完并明白了你将面对的问题之后，要准备阐述自己的观点。人人都听说过房地产的三个重要属性：位置，位置，还是位置。 同样，一位伟大的作家曾经说过沟通最重要的三个属性：清楚，清楚，还是清楚。 如果你在沟通的过程中别无他求，致力于保持表达清晰。 你不会希望自己想的是一回事，而别人做的又是另一回事。你不会希望董事会的任何人不明白你的意图，那么，你的阐述要简单、简洁和清楚。 记住一句老话，事实胜于雄辩。 如果你的行动与你宣扬的价值观和目标不符，世界上的任何演讲、备忘录和使命宣言都将变得一无是处。 你不可能榨干公司的钱来支付你的高额工资，却要求大家具备奉献精神，这样还能建立一个持久的企业。 使你的言论真实可信的最好方法，是将其落实到你的日常生活中。

企业的长久生命力不只是建立在利润和政策之上。 每一个拥有百年历史的公司最看重企业的品质。 在一个法律的世界里，任何企业都不能长时间逃避规则。 要让你的企业持续几百年，就要以坚实的伦理道德奠基。 公平和正义的定义大相径庭，不管它们对你来说意味着什么，有一个通用测试可以检验你是否越轨了。 这一检验是这样的：你是否想让大家都读到描述你行为的新闻报道？ 你可以用它来测试你自己的行为，或你的领导层伙伴和员工的行为。

家族企业成长为各种各样的企业。 有些规模很小，从来没有超

in your communication, strive to be clear. You don't want people signing up for one course of action when you intend another. And you don't want anyone on board who doesn't know where you are headed. Be simple, be brief, and be clear. Remember the old statement that actions speak louder than words. All the speeches, memos and statements in the world won't amount to much if your behavior doesn't exemplify the values and objectives you want to promote. You can't call for the sacrifices required to build an enduring company while you are draining the corporate coffers to pay yourself a rich salary. The best way to make your communications is to embody them in your everyday life.

Long business life is built on more than profits and policies. At the heart of every centuries-old company is a core of character. We exist in a world of law, and no enterprise can expect to skirt the rules for long. To exist for centuries, set up your company on a firm basis of behavior. Definitions of fairness and justice vary widely, but whatever they mean to you, there is a universal test to indicate when you may be about to go outside the lines. That test is this: Would you want to read or see a news story describing your behavior for the world? You can use this to test your own behavior and that of your fellow leaders and employees.

Family businesses grow into all sorts of enterprises. Some are simple and never expand beyond a single location. Others the globe and have interests in a broad variety of fields. Whatever your business grows into, it will benefit from having a strong foundation. And without that robust footing, it may never grow to maturity at all and wind up as just another sad story of a short-lived family firm.

(1,028 words)

出某个范围。 另一些企业遍布全球，并在多个领域有利益往来。无论你的企业发展到什么程度，有一个坚实的基础它都会受益匪浅。 基础不牢固的话，它或许根本就不可能走向成熟，结局就像又一个短命的家族企业讲述的悲惨故事。

知识链接 🔍

The Hoshi Ryokan 法师旅馆。法师旅馆即日本的粟津温泉，创建于718年，距今已经有1 300多年的经营历史，由粟津家族经营，目前的老板是第46代传人。相传白山的神向一名归山修行的僧侣显灵，指引他山脚下有一处神奇的地下温泉，僧侣听闻后下山探勘，与村民一同挖掘温泉，并指示弟子在旁盖起这座旅社。法师旅馆目前拥有一百间房间，云烟氤氲的温泉、古意的建筑与传统日式待客之道，让旅客们仿佛走进了历史的长河。

题　记

　　谈判是一门让他人为了他们自己的原因按你的方法行事的艺术。三维谈判将这门艺术发挥到了极致。三维谈判者不只是按照规定的方法来做游戏，他们是建立游戏的大师，并且改变规则，以求最优结果。肯尼科特铜业公司在与智利政府的谈判中曾深陷困境：要么接受智利政府的条款要么被剥夺经营权。如果他们采用一维谈判的方式，只考虑人际过程，包括诱劝、文化敏感性、研究报价等，无疑血本无归；如果他们采用二维谈判的方式，主张创造价值的实质，即设计能创造持续价值的协议框架，也难免败走麦城。幸运的是，他们采用了三维谈判的方式，在画出买卖关系图、全面评估各方利益并决定最佳替代方案后，成功诱导智利政府为了自身的原因选择了肯尼科特铜业公司想要的结果。

3-D Negotiation: Playing the Whole Game

Savvy① negotiators not only play their cards well, they design the game in their favor even before they get to the table. What stands between you and the yes you want? In our analysis of hundreds of negotiations, we've uncovered barriers in three complementary dimensions: The first is tactics; the second is deal design; and the third is setup. Each dimension is crucial, but many negotiators and much of the negotiation literature fixate② on only the first two.

For instance, most negotiation books focus on how executives can master tactics — interactions at the bargaining table. The common barriers to yes in this dimension include a lack of trust between parties, poor communication, and negotiators' "hardball" attitudes. So the books offer useful tips on reading body language, adapting your style to the bargaining situation, listening actively, framing your case persuasively, deciding on offers and counteroffers, managing deadlines, countering

---

① savvy ['sævi] *n.* 机智
② fixate ['fikseit] *vi.* 注视

三维谈判法：玩转整个游戏

机智的谈判者们不仅要玩好自己手中的牌，而且在他们走到谈判桌之前，就已经设计好了对己有利的谈判框架。 在谈判中你和你想得到的结果之间存在什么障碍呢？ 经过分析许许多多的谈判案例，我们从三个互补的维度发现了这些障碍：其一是谈判战术；其二是方案设计；其三是谈判设置。 每一维都是很关键的，但是很多谈判者以及大量的谈判文献只是将注意力放在前二维上。

举例来说，大多数谈判著作将焦点聚集在怎样使谈判人员在谈判桌前能够掌握谈判的战术互动。 在这一维度阻碍谈判成功的普遍障碍包括谈判各方缺少信任、沟通不良以及谈判者态度"强硬"。因此这些著作在很多方面给出了有益的建议，如：推敲对方的肢体语言，调整风格以与讨价还价的环境相适应，积极地聆听，使自己的方案更具说服力，决定发盘及还盘，制定最后期限，反对肮脏的谈判伎俩，避免文化差异带来的尴尬，等等。

谈判的第二个维度，即方案设计，也备受关注，或者说，谈判者有能力在谈判桌上制订出创造持续价值方案。 当一个方案不能给谈判各方提供足够的价值或当方案的结构无法让谈判各方达成共识时，有效的二维谈判者必须发掘潜在的经济或非经济的价值源泉，

dirty tricks, avoiding cross-cultural gaffes①, and so on.

The second dimension, that of deal design — or negotiators' ability to draw up a deal at the table that creates lasting value — also receives attention. When a deal does not offer enough value to all sides, or when its structure won't allow for success, effective 2-D negotiators work to diagnose underlying sources of economic and noneconomic value and then craft agreements that can unlock that value for the parties. Does some sort of trade between sides make sense and, if so, on what terms? Should it be a staged agreement, perhaps with contingencies and risk-sharing provisions? A deal with a more creative concept and structure? One that meets ego needs as well as economic ones?

Beyond the interpersonal and deal design challenges executives face in 1-D and 2-D negotiations lie the 3-D obstacles — flaws in the negotiating setup itself. Common problems in this often-neglected third dimension include negotiating with the wrong parties or about the wrong set of issues, involving parties in the wrong sequence or at the wrong time, as well as incompatible or unattractive no-deal options. 3-D negotiators, however, reshape the scope and sequence of the game itself to achieve the desired outcome. Acting entrepreneurially, away from the table, they ensure that the right parties are approached in the right order to deal with the right issues, by the right means, at the right time, under the right set of expectations, and facing the right no-deal options.

Former U. S. trade representative Charlene Barshefsky, who has negotiated with hundreds of companies, governments, and nongovernmental organizations to spearhead deals on goods, services,

---

① gaffe [gæf] *n.* 过失

并通过更改原方案向对方提供这些价值。 双方之间的某些交易有意义吗？ 若有的话，条款又是什么？ 它应该是一个分期协定，或许有意外事件和风险分担条款吗？ 还是一个更具创造性概念和结构的协定？ 抑或一个既满足经济需求，又满足自我需求的协定？

谈判人员除了面对一维和二维谈判层面的人际关系和方案设计的挑战，他们还面临三维层面的谈判障碍，即谈判设置本身的缺陷。 在这个常常被忽视的三维谈判方面，普遍存在的问题包括：与错误的谈判对象进行谈判或者涉及一些错误的谈判条款，谈判各方的谈判顺序安排不合理，或谈判时机不当，此外还有不相容的或没有吸引力的无交易选择。 然而，三维谈判论将整个谈判范围和谈判顺序进行了改组，并能获得理想的结果。 以企业家的方式，在谈判前就确保了谈判是在正确的时间，与正确的对象，按照合理的顺序，就合理的条款，通过适当的方式，在合理的谈判预期下，面对合理的无交易选择进行的。

美国前贸易谈判代表沙琳·巴尔舍夫斯基曾与数百家公司、政府和非政府组织在物资、服务和知识产权方面进行过谈判。 她成功总结了三维谈判法的特点："在谈判桌上，策略只是理顺工作。 许多人误认为，在你面对谈判对手时，假定最有希望的可能情形是必要的，然而，离开谈判桌，策略只不过是基本内容和没有意义的努力。 其实，当你知道你需要什么，并将一个范围更广的对策放在那儿的时候，谈判策略就会如涌泉般川流不息。"

当三维谈判领域存在障碍时，即使在谈判中拥有卓越人际沟通技巧的谈判经理也可能会失败。 20 世纪 60 年代，肯尼科特铜业公司在智利有个长期性低使用费的合同，协议规定了其对智利萨尔瓦

and intellectual property, characterizes successful 3-D negotiations this way: "Tactics at the table are only the cleanup work. Many people mistake tactics for the underlying substance and the relentless① efforts away from the table that are needed to set up the most promising possible situation once you face your counterpart. When you know what you need and you have put a broader strategy in place, then negotiating tactics will flow."

Even managers who possess superior interpersonal skills in negotiations can fail when the barriers to agreement fall in the 3-D realm. During the 1960s, Kennecott Copper's long-term, low-royalty contract governing its huge El Teniente mine in Chile was at high risk of renegotiation; the political situation in Chile had changed drastically since the contract was originally drawn up, rendering the terms of the deal unstable. Chile had what appeared to be a very attractive walk away option—or in negotiation lingo, a BATNA (best alternative to negotiated agreement). By unilateral action, the Chilean government could radically change the financial terms of the deal or even expropriate the mine. Kennecott's BATNA appeared poor: Submit to new terms or be expropriated.

Imagine that Kennecott had adopted a 1-D strategy focusing primarily on interpersonal actions at the bargaining table. Using that approach, Kennecott's management team would assess the personalities of the ministers with whom it would be negotiating. It would try to be culturally sensitive, and it might choose elegant restaurants in which to meet. Indeed, Kennecott's team did take such sensible actions. But that approach

---

① relentless [ri'lentlis] *adj.* 无情的

多尼恩特大煤矿的使用权，当时，该协议面临着重新谈判的高风险：从最初签订协议以来，智利国内的政治形势发生了剧烈的变化，最初签订的协议也处于不稳定的状态。很显然智利政府在谈判中具有很大的优势——用谈判术语，就是达成谈判协议的最佳选择方案（BATNA）。智利政府可能单方面采取行动而彻底改变协议中的金融条款或者甚至没收矿产经营权。肯尼科特公司在谈判中的境地很糟糕：要么接受新条款要么被剥夺经营权。

可以想象，若肯尼科特公司在谈判桌前只采用一维谈判方法，将重点集中在人际关系上会是什么结果。如果采用这种方法，肯尼科特铜业公司的管理层可能会对和他们进行谈判的部长们进行人身攻击。当然也可以尝试从文化的角度明智地处理，让那些部长们入住高档宾馆，以满足他们的需求。实际上，肯尼科特铜业公司正是采取了这种明智的举动。但是，考虑到公司面临威胁的现实状况，这种方法并不足以让人们对谈判前景抱有希望。智利的政府官员似乎掌控着整个局面：他们不需要肯尼科特公司经营铜矿厂，这个国家有自己的富有经验的经营者和工程师。肯尼科特铜业公司的双手似乎被束缚了：他们既不能搬走矿场，也不能控制下游的经营行为，或者说是经销这种有价值的金属；也没有任何现实的可能性，像以前那样寻求美国舰队的保护。

幸运的是，肯尼科特铜业公司采取了三维谈判方式，这对即将到来的谈判最为有利。谈判小组采取了六个步骤，同时改变了谈判的范围。首先，令智利政府有点受宠若惊的是，肯尼科特铜业公司将铜矿的大部分股权出让给他们。其二，加大出让的甜头，公司提议，用出让股权的收益和一家进出口银行的贷款资助铜矿扩大生产

wasn't promising enough given the threatening realities of the situation. Chile's officials seemed to hold all the cards: They didn't need Kennecott to run the mine; the country had its own experienced managers and engineers. And Kennecott's hands seemed tied: It couldn't move the copper mine, nor did it have a lock on downstream processing or marketing of the valuable metal, nor any realistic prospect, as in a previous era, of calling in the U.S. fleet.

Fortunately for Kennecott, its negotiators adopted a 3-D strategy and set up the impending① talks most favorably. The team took six steps and changed the playing field altogether. First, somewhat to the government's surprise, Kennecott offered to sell a majority equity interest in the mine to Chile. Second, to sweeten that offer, the company proposed using the proceeds from the sale of equity, along with money from an Export-Import Bank loan, to finance a large expansion of the mine. Third, it induced the Chilean government to guarantee this loan and make the guarantee subject to New York state law. Fourth, Kennecott insured as much as possible of its assets under a U.S. guarantee against expropriation. Fifth, it arranged for the expanded mine's output to be sold under long-term contracts with North American and European customers. And sixth, the collection rights to these contracts were sold to a consortium② of European, U.S., and Japanese financial institutions.

(905 words)

---

① impending [im'pendiŋ] *adj.* 迫在眉睫的
② consortium [kən'sɔtiəm] *n.* 团体

规模。 其三，他们诱使智利政府为银行贷款担保，并提请纽约州立法保护。 其四，为其尽可能多的资产在美国进行"防没收"保护的投保。 其五，通过长期合同，将铜矿扩张后的矿产品出售给北美和欧洲的客户。 其六，将这些合同的收益权出售给由欧洲、美国和日本金融机构组成的团体。

知识链接

Kennecott Copper 肯尼科特铜业公司。美国肯尼科特铜业公司运营着全球最大的露天铜矿——肯尼科特铜矿，该铜矿位于美国盐湖城奥克尔山脉的东部。肯尼科特铜矿每年生产大约 30 万吨铜。

题　记

　　商务预约是商务文化重要的组成部分之一，对预约技巧的掌握和控制能够改善一个商务人员的形象，甚至有时候能够帮助企业提高签约谈判的成功率。商务预约需要遵时守约，包括提前设定议程，为约会提供时间和日期选择，为事前准备和事后情况说明安排时间，以及实时更新约会日程。商务预约需要遵法守纪，包括务必确认你的确需要会面，尽量减少行程时间以及限制被邀请者的人数。商务预约需要诚信为本，包括避免华而不实的软件应用，区分个人约会和商务约会，以及最后的确认。比尔·盖茨的名言"企业竞争是员工素质的竞争"体现了商业社会竞争的激烈程度，商务预约的卓越能力就是展示员工良好优雅的专业形象的一个平台。

Improving Your Appointment Setting Skills

No matter what business you are in, the odds are that you spend at least some time in appointments. Your appointments may be big group meetings, one-on-ones, or even job interviews. You may even be skipping the face-to-face aspect of meeting and be taking conference calls or using Skype[1]. No matter what type of meeting you've scheduled, though, these tips can help you improve your appointment setting skills.

Set agendas ahead of time. Knowing what you plan to accomplish in a meeting can help you decide how long to plan to stay at that appointment — assuming you can keep to your agenda. It can be hard to get other people to stay on track, but no one really wants to spend all day in a single appointment. Furthermore, completing an agreed upon agenda is really the only way to be sure when your meeting is over.

Offer time and date options for appointments. Rather than going through a lengthy back and forth, either on the phone or via email, pick

---

① Skype *n.* 网络电话

改善预约技巧

　　不管你从事什么商业活动，花时间约会可能是必不可少的事。大集团的会议预约，一对一的预约，甚或是面试预约，这些都有可能。你甚至可以跳过会议的面对面环节，使用电话会议或网络电话等手段预约。无论你计划召开什么类型的会议，这些技巧可以帮助你提高设定预约的能力。

　　提前设定议程。如果你可以遵守议程，那么了解你希望在会面中要达到什么结果可以帮助你决定约会需要多长时间。很难让其他人坚持到最后，但真没有人想整天约会。此外，达成议程的共识是确定何时结束会面的真正的唯一途径。

　　为约会提供时间和日期选择。与其经历一个漫长的来回，还不如通过电话或电子邮件，选择两三个适合你的预约时间，并通知预约对方。如果你打交道的群体人比较多，几乎可以肯定只有一种选择不适合某些人，多项选择是达成共识的快得多的方式。

　　避免华而不实的软件应用。虽然市面上有一些非常时髦的预约设置软件，但要尽量避免使用这些与众不同的东西。聚会或大型会议是这个规则的例外。一般而言，使用这些应用软件需要花费比它们的价值更多的时间，对新用户来说，有一个学习曲线，他们必须

two or three appointment times that work for you and present them to the other half of your appointment. If you're dealing with a larger group, it's almost guaranteed that at least one option won't work for someone, and having multiple options is a much faster way to reach consensus.

Avoid fancy software applications. While there is some very snazzy① appointment setting software out there, try to avoid using anything out of the ordinary. The exception to this rule is parties or very large meetings. In general, using these applications take more time than they're worth — there's a learning curve for new users, and having to visit a site to respond can take double the time of replying to an email. However, when you're trying to coordinate large groups of people, using an application can provide a central location rather than sending out huge batches② of emails.

Make sure you really need a meeting. Plenty of appointments are set for simple things like handing over a document for approval. Unless that document is short enough to be completely examined during the meeting, it might be more worthwhile to drop off the document and come back later to answer questions and handle the approval process. Before actually setting your appointment, think about whether the matter could be handled in a faster way.

Minimize travel time. One of the reasons that appointments eat up so

---

① snazzy ['snæzi] *adj.* 时髦的
② batch [bætʃ] *n.* 一批

访问特定的网站并回复，这要花费比回复电子邮件多一倍的时间。然而，当你试图协调一大群人的时候，使用应用程序可以提供一个中央单元，避免发送大批次的电子邮件。

务必确认你的确需要会面。大量的预约都只是办一些简单的事情，例如交一份待批准的文件。除非该文件很短，足以在会面期间审查完成，否则就将文件暂时搁置，稍后再转头回答问题并处理审批流程，这种做法可能更值得考虑。在实际设定预约之前，想一想这件事是否还有更快的处理方式。

尽量减少行程时间。会面吞噬了我们大量的日常时间，原因之一就是必要的行程耗损。我们不得不拜访客户的办公室、咖啡馆或根本不愿前往的约会地点。我们可以建议，在我们自己的所在地会面、中途会面，或者完全取消个人会面，这样可以最大限度地减少这一投入。选择电话或视频会议的方式往往能帮你解决跨城镇会议的预约需求。

为事前准备和事后情况说明安排时间。设定约会时，想一想你可能需要为它准备什么，如回顾一下报告，准备一下介绍，或熨一下衬衫等。在实际约会前，为这些活动中的每一项安排出时间。在约会前，为最后时刻的任何细节安排一个 15 分钟的预备时间也是值得的。这些做法同样适用于事后情况说明：你可能在会面后还有某些后续处理任务。会面后至少安排几分钟的时间，确保你有足够时间检查笔记是否完整，至少要将任何一项在当时无法完成的后续工作列入你的日程表。

区分个人约会和商务约会。我们中的许多人试着把我们办公外的所有约会纳入一天。这种做法忽视了可能发生的情况，如果恰好

much time in our calendars is the necessity of travel. We have to travel to clients' offices, coffee shops or wherever the heck① we're meeting. We can minimize that commitment by suggesting that we meet at our own locations, meet halfway, or skip meeting in person altogether. Options like telephone calls or video conferencing can often handle all the requirements of that appointment you were going to drive across town for.

Schedule time for both preparation and debriefing②. When you set your appointment, think about what you might need to do to prepare for it — review a report, prepare a presentation or iron your shirt — and schedule time for each of those activities before your actual appointment. It's also worthwhile to schedule a fifteen-minute prep session just before your appointment for any last minute details. Same goes for afterwards: you may have certain follow-up tasks to handle after your meeting. Scheduling at least a few minutes after an appointment guarantees that you'll have time to make sure your notes are complete and any sort of further action at least makes it on to your calendar if you can't do it then.

Separate personal and business appointments. Many of us try to load all of our out-of-the-office appointments into one day. Ignoring the problem of what happens if just one runs late, you've got the issue of trying to switch gears between the presentation you just gave to a client and the shot the doctor's waiting to give you. That sort of mental switch up

---

① heck [hek] *n.* 地狱,糟糕的地方
② debrief [di'bri:f] *vt.* 报告

有一个约会拖延了时间，你就得想办法处理这样的问题：你向客户介绍情况和医生等待给你注射。 这种心理上的协调只会使你在处理即将来临的约会时变得更加困难。 请尝试将个人约会和商务约会安排在不同的时间。

实时更新约会日程。 如果你不是唯一一个安排自己约会的人，考虑将其他人安排进来是至关重要的。 否则，你在完成重大项目的同时，家人可能期盼与你共进晚餐。 我喜欢共享日程表，为此专门定制了谷歌日程表，但如果你依赖自己的体系，还有很多方式可以分享几乎所有类型的日程表。 约会协调人可以包括你的经理、你的另一半、你的行政助理或部门的行政助理以及一大堆其他人。

限制被邀请者的人数。 你可能并不需要整个公司的人出席进度报告会。 但你应该决定谁确实需要参加约会。 如果有人感到受冷落，通常可以在过些时候发送大量的电子邮件。 我曾经面临这样的处境，如果在任何一个设定的会议中没有将高层纳入在内，就会有人感到被排除在外。 最好的办法似乎是让他们觉得这个会议就像是一件根本不值得他们花费时间的事情。

确认一切！ 确认会面的时间和地点，议程包含什么，甚至包括如何到达会面场所。 你真正需要的是在约会前的一两天内，发送简短的电子邮件，概述一下会面的内容，而且如果一切无误，要求一个简单肯定的答复。

知识链接

Skype 网络电话。网络电话是基于 VoIP 技术的语音通信软件，与语音交换

can only make it harder to handle your later appointments. Try to schedule your personal and business appointments on different days.

Keep your appointment schedulers up to date. If you aren't the only person scheduling your appointments, it's vital to keep the others in the loop. Otherwise, your significant other might be expecting you at a family dinner at the same time you're finishing up a major project. I like shared calendars, such as Google Calendar for that very reason, but there are ways to share just about every type of calendar, if you're reliant on your own system. Appointment schedulers can include your manager, your significant other, an administrative assistant of yours or the departments and a whole host of other people.

Limit invitees. You may not need the whole company present for a progress report. Instead, decide who actually needs to be in on your appointment — you can always send out a mass email later on if people feel left out. I've been in situations before where higher ups felt left out if you didn't bring them in on every single appointment you were setting up. The best bet seems to be presenting the meeting as something that wouldn't be a valuable use of their time.

Confirm everything! Confirm when and where the meeting is, what the agenda covers, even how to get there. All you really need is a brief email a day or two before the appointment that outlines the appointment and ask for a simple yes in response if everything is correct.

(914 words)

服务器、电话网关和接点交换服务器构成完整的语音通信平台，还支持包括 USB 语音通信手柄、USB-RJ11 转换盒和 PCI-RJ11 转换卡等硬件产品，能够在以 TCP/IP 协议为基础的网络上提供 PCTOPC、PCTOPhone 和 PhoneTOPhone 的通信服务，可以满足电信运营商、宽带运营商提供通信服务和企业解决通信问题的需要。

题 记

　　在产品和公司价值定位中，品牌是个至关重要的元素。放弃老品牌资产或者躺在老品牌上不思进取，这种论调可能会亵渎神明，但有些时候变革就是势在必行。对老品牌进行重新构造、重新设计或者拆检翻修是明智之举。曾经的处理器巨人英特尔公司正逐渐走向没落，电脑中的显示屏、存储器和微处理器使用的技术变更使英特尔曾经的定位远离市场。新一代网络大亨谷歌品牌完全与当前的网络文化紧密相连，它采用多元化战略，不仅单独与网络搜索引擎对接，而且与人们在网络所做的每件事交往。谷歌品牌的辉煌见证了市场理念、品牌构建、品牌忠诚度的价值，而英特尔品牌的危机与过时的技术紧密相连。

A Wise Decision of Brands

It might be almost blasphemous① to talk about letting go of old brand equity and laying an old brand to rest, but there are times when change is needed. Reformulating and re-designing, or even overhauling an old brand can be a wise decision. If sales are flat and show no sign of growth, you'd better stop kidding yourself and hire a branding consultant.

Brands are an extremely vital element in your product and corporate value proposition. With communications so pervasive today, corporate branding and product branding are becoming fused as one. Corporate brands are increasingly powering product brands and product sales and that pose some substantial risk, as those sub brands can't be as easily re-positioned when they falter.

As time passes, culture changes, new technologies and new competing brands appear and they change the perception of value that is available in a marketplace. Old sales propositions won't fly in the face of 20 or more other competitors offering the same benefits and features. With

---

① blasphemous ['blæsfiməs] *adj.* 亵渎神祇的

品牌的明智之举

　　放弃老品牌资产或者躺在老品牌上不思进取，这种论调可能会亵渎神明，但有些时候变革就是势在必行。 对老品牌进行重新构造、重新设计或者拆检翻修是明智之举。 如果销售平平又毫无增长迹象，你最好停止欺骗自己，雇用一名品牌顾问。

　　在产品和公司价值定位中，品牌是个至关重要的元素。 随着时下沟通的普及，公司品牌和产品品牌正在融为一体。 公司品牌不断为产品品牌和产品销售注入能量，这也造成了一些重大风险，当品牌摇摇欲坠之时，子品牌也难以重新定位。

　　文化随着时间的推移变迁，新技术和新的竞争品牌不断涌现，他们改变了品牌可利用的市场价值概念。 旧的销售定位面对 20 个或者更多的能提供相似特征产品的竞争者时将不再有效。 随着文化、经济、技术以及公司的变化，老化的品牌形象和品牌资产很可能弊大于利，并最终走向终结。 过去的品牌成功可能使你的品牌和公司停留在过去。

　　与老品牌相关的问题可以在电脑产品领域找到很好的例子。 我最近买了一台新的手提电脑，因为那台旧电脑无法满足多重任务处理和其他的工作需要。 零售店提供了两种电脑以供选择：英特尔公

cultural, economic, technology changes, and corporate changes, your aging brand image and brand equity may end up doing more harm than good. Your former branding successes could leave your brand and company stuck in the past.

A good example of age related branding problem is in the realm of computer products. I recently bought a new laptop computer because my old one just couldn't keep up with my multitasking and other work needs. At the retail store, there were computers with Intel or AMD microprocessors to choose from. The key matter wasn't really microprocessor speed or capability. In the past, the Intel logo would have compelled me to buy only computers with their processors regardless of what other features were available in the computer. The Intel brand was clearly in a class by itself. Not this time. This AMD powered computer was low priced and had the memory I required along with other features such as a 100 GB hard drive, high-resolution screen, numerous ports and adapters and a long lasting battery. It only weighs a couple of pounds and the AMD logo seemed to look better too. It says: AMD Turion 64 Mobile Technology, 64 bits and mobile compatibility. Why doesn't Intel mention that on the computer they have their products in?

Laptops are hot and prices are falling. My 15-year-old nephew just bought his first laptop on eBay, since they are cheaper and more accessible. So the whole "culture" of shopping and purchasing computers has changed. Everyone is buying high-resolution screens and I was eager to ease my eyestrain from long hours of viewing everyday. The huge hard drive was great and the laptop looks good too. The old Intel

司的电脑和 AMD 公司的微处理器电脑。 问题的关键并不真正在于微处理器的速度或容量。 在过去，英特尔的标志迫使我只买内置英特尔微处理器的电脑，而不考虑该电脑的其他特性。 很显然，英特尔的品牌是独一无二的。 但这次不是这样。 这台内置 AMD 微处理器的电脑不仅价格便宜，拥有我需要的储存量，还有 100GB 的硬盘驱动、高处理频率、许多适配器，以及可以长时间使用的电池等其他特性。 电脑只有几磅重，而且 ADM 的商标似乎看起来更为醒目。 它声称：AMD Turion 64 款是专为笔记本电脑设计的 64 位移动处理器，同时支持 64 位应用和移动兼容。 为什么英特尔不在它的产品中提到这一点呢？

笔记本电脑正在热卖，且价格也在不断下降。 我那个 15 岁的侄子刚刚在易趣上买了他的第一台笔记本电脑，因为这些笔记本电脑不仅更便宜，而且购买更方便。 所以，购买电脑的整个"文化"已经发生了改变。 人人都在购买有高分辨率显示屏的电脑，我迫切希望摆脱每天长时间阅读带来的视觉疲劳。 超大型的硬盘驱动方便快捷，笔记本电脑看起来也很不错。 老牌英特尔昔日辉煌不再，其竞争对手 AMD 刚刚售出了他们的一台处理器。 这种笔记本运行良好，现在，英特尔的微处理器也并非是我购买电脑的唯一选择。

对我来说，英特尔的标识和品牌让我联想起"奔腾"电脑时代的旧时光。 当代的处理器已经发生变化，而英特尔的处理器还是在缓慢地低速运行，这个事实使情况变得更糟。 人们开始质疑英特尔品牌定位的速度优势。 电脑中的显示屏、存储器和微处理器使用的技术变更使英特尔曾经的定位远离市场。 英特尔公司的品牌促进了其新微处理器的销售，但是不管他们如何称呼这些新产品，仍然无

brand just didn't have the effect it once did, and their competitor, AMD, just sold one of their processors. The laptop is working great and now Intel processors don't dictate which computer I'll buy.

To me, the Intel logo and brand brings back memories of old Pentium computers. This is worsened by the fact that today's processors have changed and they are running at lower speeds. This confuses the speed benefit that Intel had its brand positioned around. The technology change in viewing screens, memory, and processor use in the computer has moved the market away from where Intel was positioned. The Intel corporate brand powers sales of their new processors, but they can call those new products anything they want and it won't effective my decision.

What Intel needs to do now, is to associate its processors with the features and benefits that consumers and B2B buyers make decisions upon. Computer branding is not all about the processors anymore and the old Intel brand image is deeply tied to old technology. Even the brand name Pentium is associated with the computer culture of the 90's.

Here's the issue: the old Intel brand was so successful in 90's that it's trapped Intel in a time warp. Intel needs new branding that ties it to the future, not the past. To get there, they are probably going to have to jettison① the past.

Google is a good example of modern branding and a brand that is not tied solely to web search engines. The brand is now diversified strategically

---

① jettison [ˈdʒetisn] vt. 摒弃

法影响我的购买决定。

　　将其微处理器的产品特点与消费者和企业对企业的买家制定购买决策时的利益联系起来，这就是英特尔现在需要做的工作。 电脑品牌不再完全等同于微处理器品牌，英特尔品牌以往的形象与过时的技术紧密相连。"奔腾"品牌也打上了 20 世纪 90 年代电脑文化的烙印。

　　这就是问题的所在：英特尔的老品牌在 20 世纪 90 年代是如此的成功，以致其被困于英特尔的时间隧道。 英特尔需要与未来而不是与过去接轨的新品牌。 为了达到这个目的，他们可能不得不抛弃过去。

　　谷歌是现代品牌的经典范例，该品牌不只是单独与网络搜索引擎对接。 谷歌品牌采用多元化战略，与人们在网络所做的每件事交往。 谷歌无处不在，其品牌形象完全与当前的网络文化紧密相连。谷歌不会让其普通搜索引擎的角色削弱它的品牌效应。

　　品牌经理、首席执行官和营销经理们不愿意重新思考和重新发展他们的品牌是有很多原因的。 他们不愿意走出自己的舒适带，为少量的短期利润冒险，这是最常见的原因。 有些人不愿意雇用品牌顾问，不愿花本钱调查可供选择的方案。

　　品牌专家通过研究品牌来发现它当前的问题和市场文化，并决定新品牌的资产或品牌定位是否富有成效。 有些老品牌注定要退出市场，但大多数老品牌只不过是缺乏新意和不适应目标市场。 品牌顾问可以对市场理念、品牌价值构建、品牌忠诚度发展提供至关重要的见解，发现品牌的价值定位，赋予品牌新的活力。

　　从产品到公司品牌，再到互联网上的广义品牌，品牌认证资产

to associate it with everything people are doing on the web. Google is omnipresent①, and its brand image is solely in its relevance to the current Internet culture. Google won't let its common search engine role diminish its branding power.

There's a lot of reason why brand managers, CEO's, and marketing managers resist rethinking their branding and redeveloping their brands. Most often, they don't want to leave their comfort zone and risk a short-term blip② in profit. Some don't want to make an investment in hiring a branding consultant to look at the options.

Branding experts examine a brand to discover its current problems, the culture of the marketplace, and to determine if a new brand identity or brand positioning would be fruitful. Some old brands are doomed, but most are just stale and not in tune with the target market. A branding consultant can provide crucial insight into market perception, brand value building, brand loyalty development, and to discover the brand value proposition that could breathe new life into your brands.

From product, to corporate branding to extending brands on the Internet, Brand Identity Guru provides corporate clients with brand audits, brand design, brand web design, and search engine marketing services.

(912 words)

---

① omnipresent [ɔmni'prezənt] *adj.* 无所不在的
② blip [blip] *n.* 信号

为公司的客户提供了品牌审核、品牌设计、品牌网络设计以及搜索引擎营销服务。

知识链接 🔍

Intel 英特尔。英特尔公司是全球设计和生产半导体的科技巨擘。它成立于1968 年，具有 44 年产品创新和市场领导的历史。它为全球日益发展的计算机工业提供架构模块，包括微处理器、芯片组、板卡、系统及软件等。这些产品为标准计算机架构的组成部分，业界利用这些产品为最终用户设计制造出先进的计算机。

Google 谷歌公司。谷歌是一家美国的上市公司，于 1998 年以私有股份公司的形式创立，以设计并管理一个互联网搜索引擎。谷歌公司的总部位于加利福尼亚山景城，在全球各地都设有销售和工程办事处。谷歌公司的文化价值观是"完美的搜索引擎需要做到确解用户之意，切返用户之需"。

题　记

　　韦尔奇有一句名言："如果你想让列车时速再快 10 公里，只需要加一加马力；而若想使车速增加一倍，你就必须要更换铁轨了。资产重组可以一时提高公司的生产力，但若没有文化上的改变，就无法维持高生产力的发展。"IBM 公司的企业文化是在老托马斯·沃森和小托马斯·沃森父子两代人共同生产经营中创造的，它渗透进 IBM 人的血液和骨髓，要想对其改变谈何容易。而对价值观和行为准则设置法典式的规范和僵尸般的氛围常常使成功的企业遭受重创。IBM 公司在追求伟大与卓越的过程中虽然不是十全十美，但它的企业文化仍然在剔除糟粕、吸取精华的传承中与时俱进。改变 IBM 公司的着装模式，清除强势的官僚运作机制，以及让 IBM 人重新找回自信，是他们接受在全球化环境中衍生的高度结构化和复杂化文化的崭新认知和发展动力。

The Battle to Change
Corporate Culture

Back in the early 1990s, when a person saw or heard "IBM", what words and images came to mind? "Big computers", maybe. But inevitably they would also think "big company", "conservative", "regimented", "reliable" and "dark suits and white shirts".

What's interesting is that these latter descriptions refer not to products or services but to people and a business culture. IBM may be unique in this regard; the company has been known as much for its culture as for what it made and sold. Even today if you pause and think "IBM", chances are you'll think of attributes of a kind of enterprise and its people rather than of computers or software.

Culture may be just one among several important elements in any organization's make-up and success — along with vision, strategy, marketing, financials and the like. But culture isn't just one aspect of the game at IBM — it is the game. In the end, an organization is nothing more than the collective capacity of its people to create value. Vision, strategy, marketing, financial management — any management system,

改变公司文化之战

　　回到 20 世纪 90 年代初期，人们看到或听到"IBM"时，大脑中会出现哪些词和哪些形象？ 也许是"巨型计算机"。 但是他们也会不由自主地联想起"大公司"、"传统守旧"、"循规蹈矩"、"值得信赖"以及"深色西装和白衬衫"这样一些词汇。

　　有趣的是，这些时尚的词汇与产品或服务无关，它们只是对员工和企业文化进行了描述。 IBM 在这方面也许非同寻常，公司的文化如同它所制造和销售的产品一样大名鼎鼎。 就是在今天，你停下来想一想"IBM"，很可能会想到这个公司及其员工的特征，不会想到计算机和软件。

　　公司的架构和成功包括愿景、策略、市场交易和金融等方面，文化也许只是其中的几个要素之一。 但文化不仅仅是 IBM 公司游戏的一个方面——它本身就是游戏。 公司最终不过是人们创造价值的合力。 事实上，任何管理系统，包括愿景、策略、市场交易和金融管理，都可以让你把握正确的方向，并在前进的路上助你一程。 任何一家单位，无论是企业、政府、教育机构、医疗机构，还是人类

in fact — can set you on the right path and can carry you for a while. But no enterprise — whether in business, government, education, healthcare or any area of human endeavour — will succeed over the long haul if those elements aren't part of its DNA.

Inevitably, though, as the world changes, the rules, guidelines and customs that go to make up a culture may lose their connection to what the enterprise is all about. A perfect example was the IBM dress code. It was well known throughout business circles that IBM sales people — or, for that matter, any IBM employee — wore very formal business attire. This was fine while all corporate executives wore dark suits and white shirts. However, as the years went by customers changed how they dressed at work and few of the technical buyers in corporations showed up in white and blue. But IBM's dress code marched on. When this dress code was abolished, it got an extraordinary amount of attention in the press. Some thought it was an action of great portent①. In fact, it was one of the easiest decisions IBM made — or, rather, didn't make; it wasn't really a decision. It didn't replace one dress code with another. It simply applied common sense: dress according to the circumstances of your day and recognize who you will be with customers, government leaders or just colleagues in the labs.

---

① portent['pɔːtent] n. 征兆

活动的其他领域，都必须将这些要素作为公司发展基因的一部分，否则就不能维持长时间的成功。

　　然而，随着世界的变化，构成企业文化的规则、指导方针和习俗会不可避免地与企业的全面发展失去关系。 IBM 公司着装规范就是最经典的例子。 任何一位 IBM 公司的员工，都穿着很正式的职业装，这在商界无人不晓。 行政人员穿黑套装和白衬衫固然精神抖擞，但是随着时间的推移，客户在工作中的着装发生了改变，来公司购买技术产品的消费者极少穿黑白套装，但是 IBM 公司的着装还是一成不变。 IBM 公司废除这种着装规范时，引起了大量媒体的特别关注。 有人认为，这种举动是个好兆头。 其实这是 IBM 公司所做的最轻松的决定之一，或者说不是做决定，它不算是一个真正的决定。 它不是用一种着装规范代替另一种着装规范。 它不过利用了常识，即根据当天所处的环境和将要面对的客户、政府官员抑或只是实验室同事来着装。

　　对价值观和行为准则设置这种法典式的规范和僵尸般的氛围常常使成功的企业遭受重创，这是一个他们独有的难题。 许多过去历经低潮的成功企业，包括 IBM、希尔斯、通用汽车、柯达、施乐等，也许对所处环境的变化有着清醒的认识。 他们也许对外界的变化能够形成概念和表达需求，甚至可以采取一些策略，但他们无法改变在不同的环境中衍生的高度结构化和复杂的文化。

　　"官僚主义"一词也许在现今的许多机构里呈现贬义色彩。 事

This codification①, this rigor② mortis③ that sets in around values and behaviors, is a problem unique to — and often devastating for — successful enterprises. Many successful companies that have fallen on hard times in the past — including IBM, Sears, General Motors, Kodak, Xerox and many others — saw perhaps quite clearly the changes in their environment. They were probably able to conceptualize and articulate the need for change and perhaps even develop strategies for it. But their inability to change highly structured, sophisticated cultures that had been born in a different world.

The word "bureaucracy" has taken on a negative connotation in most institutions today. The truth is that no large enterprise can work without bureaucracy. Bureaucrats, or staff people, provide co-ordination among disparate line organizations; establish and enforce corporate-wide strategies that allow the enterprise to avoid duplication, confusion and conflict; and provide highly specialized skills that cannot be duplicated, because of cost or simply the shortage of available resources.

These functions were all critical to an organization like IBM. Co-ordination was critical because IBM had a four-way matrix: geography, product, customer and solutions. The company also desperately needed corporate-wide standards for many aspects — e. g., commonality of

---

① codification[ˌkɔdifiˈkeiʃən] *n.* 法律成文化
② rigor[ˈrigɔː] *n.* 僵直
③ mortis [ˈmɔːtis] *n.* 莫蒂斯人

实上任何一家大公司离了官僚主义都无法运作。 官僚管理者或员工可以给毫不相干的直线集权型企业组织提供协调，为了使企业避免重复、混乱和冲突而建立和实施广泛的公司战略，并提供无法复制的尖端专业技能来克服成本或可用资源短缺等因素造成的影响。

对于 IBM 这样的公司，这些功能缺一不可。 由于 IBM 公司的结构呈地理位置、产品、客户和解决方案等四个方形矩阵，协调就显得至关重要。 公司还亟须在很多方面制定广泛的企业标准，如为遍布全球的客户运作提供具有世界各地共性的产品，建立通用的人力资源管理流程，推动公司人才快速而有效地流动，以备随时需要之用。 考虑到全球性的跨国公司的复杂性，整个公司显然需要专业资源，如品牌专家和知识产权律师。

IBM 的问题不是官僚主义的存在，而是它的规模和如何使用这种规模。 在 IBM 公司的"否定"文化中，步兵是 IBM 公司的主要工作人员，而这种文化渲染的是部门之间相互竞争的多方在不同阶段的冲突中掩盖彼此的行为，希望阻止其他的 IBM 人闯入自己的领地。 他们没有促进协调，而是设置障碍，保护自己的领地。 例如，大量的员工无休止地辩论和商讨 IBM 公司部门之间的转让定价条款，没有推动产品转移给客户的无缝对接。 因为管理人员不相信跨部门的同事可以做好工作，公司各个层面的员工部门如出一辙。大量的人踊跃参加精简部门问题的决议会，因为每个人都需要到场，保护他或她的地盘。

products around the world for customers who operate globally; and common HR processes so the company could move talent quickly and effectively whenever it was needed. And, given the complexity of a highly technical, global company, the entire company clearly needed specialized resources, e.g., branding specialists and intellectual property lawyers.

The problem at IBM was not the presence of bureaucracy, but its size and how it was used. In IBM's culture of "no" — a multi-phased conflict in which units competed with one another, hid things from one an other and wanted to control access to their territory from other IBMers — the foot soldiers were IBM staff people. Instead of facilitating co-ordination, they manned the barricades and protected the borders. For example, huge staffs spent countless hours debating and managing transfer pricing terms between IBM units instead of facilitating a seamless transfer of products to customers. Staff units were duplicated at every level of the organization because no managers trusted any cross-unit colleagues to carry out the work. Meetings to decide issues that cut across units were attended by throngs of people, because everyone needed to be present to protect his or her turf.

The net result of all this jockeying for position was a very powerful bureaucracy working at all levels of the company — tens of thousands trying to protect the prerogatives, resources and profits of their units; and thousands more trying to bestow order and standards on the mob. Frankly, if IBM could have chosen not to tackle the IBM culture head-on, it probably wouldn't have. We could take a fresh look at the business

占据有利位置的最终结果是公司各个层面出现非常强势的官僚运作机制，即成千上万的人在维护其部门的特权、资源和利润，数以千计的更多的人试图为一群乌合之众设立秩序和标准。 坦率地说，如果 IBM 公司没有选择正面处理它的文化问题，也许就不会有今天的面貌。 我们可以用新的视角来看待企业，制定良好的战略系统，要么投资新的企业，要么使成本结构处于良好的状态。 也许所有需要解决的最棘手的问题是 IBM 公司的员工接受这种文化渗透。许多人以等级制为借口，不愿意承担个人责任的结果。 他们没有抓住可利用的资源和权力，只是等待老板告诉他们要做什么——他们在等待授权。

最后，文化变革的最深层次目标是使 IBM 人重新相信自己——相信他们有能力决定他们自己的命运，相信他们已经知道他们需要知道的东西。 要将他们从沮丧的低迷中拯救出来，提醒他们是谁——见鬼，你就是 IBM 人！ ——使他们协同思考和行动，成为如饥似渴、好奇而富有主动精神的人。 尽管很难维系这种平衡，但人们还是很乐观。 这个曾经沉睡的巨人的内部已经激流涌动。 它的人民再度觉醒，意识到他们是谁，他们能做什么。 此外，我们今天所处的市场是有史以来最活跃、最具竞争力的全球经济市场，它让我们受益匪浅。 只要 IBM 人保持对外部的关注，他们就会与世界同步。

and make good strategic calls or invest in new businesses or get the cost structure in shape. Perhaps the toughest nut of all to crack was getting IBM employees to accept that invitation. Many used hierarchy as a crutch① and were reluctant to take personal responsibility for outcomes. Instead of grabbing available resources and authority, they waited for the boss to tell them what to do — they delegated up.

In the end, the deepest culture-change goal was to induce IBMers to believe in themselves again — to believe that they had the ability to determine their own fate, and that they already knew what they needed to know. It was to shake them out of their depressed stupor②, remind them of who they were — you're IBM, damn it! — and get them thinking and acting collaboratively, as hungry, curious self-starters. Sustaining that balance will be tough, but people are optimistic. Something has stirred inside this once sleeping giant. Its people have been reawakened to who they are, what they are, what they can do. Besides, the marketplace we are now living in — the most dynamic, competitive, global economy in recorded history — will help. As long as IBMers remain focused outward, the world will keep them on their toes.

(1,078 words)

---

① crutch[krʌtʃ] *n.* 精神寄托
② stupor['stjuːpə] *n.* 恍惚

知识链接 🔍

Sears 希尔斯。美国最大的百货连锁店希尔斯创立于 1886 年，至今已 123 年。希尔斯创立之初以卖手表起家，并于 1893 年成立现在大家所熟悉的 Sears，Roebuck and Co.，主要的营业活动为从事邮购及百货业务。2005 年，美国 K-mart 兼并 Sears 百货，组成名为 Sears Holding Corporation Ltd （SHCL）的控股公司，合并后的公司为美国第三大零售公司，拥有 3 500 家店，年营业额约 550 亿美元，市场总值为 200 亿美元。

题　记

　　狄龙模型从一个全新的角度向人们阐释了品牌效应：一方面，产品的物理属性并不代表一个可持续的市场优势，随着时间的推移，一旦被竞争对手模仿并超越，专利权将会消耗殆尽，买家说不出来类似产品之间的差别，而且当产品效应消退时，留下来的只是人们对品牌的联想；另一方面，由于许多品牌的建立出现在其营销活动的过程中，所以认识到社会背景下产品的用途比拥有一种属性更加重要。这种把品牌效应和品牌资产分离开来理解品牌效应的方法，强调了消费者对品牌的信任更胜于产品本身的观点，可口可乐和星巴克的畅销就是品牌带给消费者正面、积极联想的最佳范例。

What's in a Brand Name

Imagine buying Coca-Cola from a vending machine and getting an unmarked can of pop with no familiar logo, no red-and-white markings, nothing to identify it as a soft drink, let alone as the Real Thing. Would that product still be Coke as we know it? And would consumers purchase this product without its world-famous packaging?

The truth is, the only physical product that the Coca-Cola Company sells is soft drink syrup to bottlers — not the bottles and cans of Coke that consumers buy. The company's greatest success comes from selling its brand, says William Dillon, associate dean for academic affairs and Herman W. Lay Professor of Marketing and Statistics in SMU's Cox School of Business. Dillon's research helps to differentiate among the threads of association and bias that affect consumer product choices and enables companies to make sense of where and why their products achieve their market positions.

To find these results, Dillon says, it's important to distinguish among the factors involved in consumer decisions and how they affect aspects of a brand's identity. He first makes the distinction between brand equity and brand valuation. Brand equity, like equity in a home, "is meant to reflect appreciation — the good things and positive associations that accrue① because

---

① accrue [əˈkruː] vi. 增长

品牌的内涵是什么

　　想象一下，从自动售货机里买可口可乐，拿到一罐没有熟悉商标的无标记汽水，没有红白相间的成交价格记录，没法把它定性为软性饮料，更不用说他们是真品了。 这种产品还是我们熟知的可口可乐吗？ 没有举世闻名的包装，消费者还会购买此产品吗？

　　事实上，可口可乐公司销售的唯一实体产品是瓶装的软饮料糖浆，而不是消费者购买的装可口可乐的瓶子和易拉罐。 美国南方卫理公会大学考克斯商学院负责学术事务的副主任威廉·狄龙和市场营销及统计学教授赫尔曼·莱认为，该公司最大的成功在于出售其品牌。 狄龙的研究有助于区分影响消费者产品选择的复杂因素和偏爱，使公司明确他们的产品在何处、以及为什么实现其市场地位。

　　狄龙指出，要得到这些结果，重要的是分辨消费者做决策时考虑的因素以及它们如何影响品牌的身份。 他首先区分了品牌资产和品牌价值。 狄龙认为，品牌资产如同家庭资产，"目的是反映增值，即积累好的东西和积极的联想，因为品牌已经兑现了它声明的承诺"。"资产是品牌的财富。"根据《商业周刊》公布的国际品牌年度排名前 100 位的品牌名单认定，品牌价值试图为这种资产添加一个可衡量的价值。

the brand has delivered on its stated promises, " Dillon says. "Equity is the brand's asset." Brand valuation, as determined through such exercises as Interbrand's annual top 100 brands list published in Business Week, attempts to attach a measurable value to that asset.

Typically, one looks at the market share of the brand and the price premium that the brand commands. The notion is that brands that have created equity command a price premium in the marketplace. Hence consumers may pay $ 1.89 for a cup of Starbucks coffee when they could purchase the same volume for about 69 cents at another coffee shop. Most equity research tries to assess the strength of a brand through price premium or market share.

One simple way of assessing this is to "equalize the products, label them, and then see how much someone is willing to pay, " Dillon says. For example, a coffee company may put the same brew in two containers — one labeled "Starbucks" and the other, perhaps, "Bill's Fresh Coffee." If consumers prefer the Starbucks coffee and will pay more for it simply because of the label, their choices appear to be determined by their positive associations with the Starbucks' name.

Such methods encounter obstacles, however, when it comes to finding an unbranded alternative to use as a base case. Typically, the benchmark is a product with no brand effect, such as a store brand or an unmarked generic. "But there really aren't unbranded products any more, " Dillon says. Many in-house and regional brands have established strong presences in the modern marketplace.

To manage such dilemmas, Dillon separates the brand effect from the product effect. The brand effect demonstrates that a consumer will pay extra for a cup of Starbucks coffee simply because it's Starbucks, and not because the product is intrinsically better. On the other hand, if

人们通常着眼于品牌的市场份额和品牌支配的价格溢价。 这种概念表明，创造了资产的品牌在市场上控制着价格溢价。 因此，消费者可能会花 1.89 美元买一杯星巴克咖啡，而在另一家咖啡店花大约 69 美分就可以买到等量的咖啡。 大多数资产研究试图通过价格溢价或市场份额评估一个品牌的力度。

狄龙说，评估品牌力度的一个简单方法是"在相同的产品上贴不同的标签，然后看看人们愿意出多少钱购买"。 例如，一家咖啡公司可能会把同样的啤酒放在两个集装箱，一个标有"星巴克"，另一个也许标有"比尔新鲜咖啡"。 如果消费者偏爱星巴克咖啡，为了它的商标也愿意付更多的钱，那么他们对星巴克品牌产生的积极联想似乎决定了他们的选择。

但是，在寻找一个无品牌的替代品作基准时，这种方法就遇到了障碍。 一般来说，基准是一种没有品牌效应的产品，如商店品牌或无注册商标产品。 狄龙说，"实际上已经没有无注册商标的产品了"。 许多内部和区域品牌都已经在现代市场强势扩大了影响。

为了解决这种进退两难的困境，狄龙将品牌效应和产品效应区分开来。 品牌效应显示，消费者为一杯星巴克咖啡支付额外的费用只是因为它是星巴克，而不是因为这种产品本质上更好。 另一方面，如果消费者认为星巴克采用了高品质的咖啡豆，或者其酿造方法生产出了口味更好的咖啡，那么他们的选择就是基于产品效应——星巴克咖啡从根本上优于其竞争者。

消费者可能依据产品某个讨人喜欢的特性给它评级，如止痛药的效力、牙膏防蛀程度的等级都是从 1 至 10。 狄龙的模型把消费者的评级分为两个部分：专有品牌联想（BSA）或者说属性和品牌之间

consumers believe that Starbucks uses a higher-quality bean, or that its brewing methods produce a better-tasting coffee, their choices are based on the product effect — a perception that Starbucks coffee is fundamentally better than that of its competitors.

A consumer may rate a product on a favorable characteristic — strength for a pain reliever, or decay prevention for a toothpaste — on a scale of 1 to 10. Dillon's models separate the customer's rating into two components: the Brand-Specific Association (BSA), or the actual linkage between the attribute and the brand; and the General Brand Impression (GBI), or the consumer's general like or dislike of the brand itself. This breakdown allows companies to understand the weight that general impressions can carry in driving consumer choice.

A benefit of Dillon's model is that it accommodates brand ratings as they typically are gathered in customer tracking surveys — for example, the 1-to-10 unfavorable-or-favorable scale. In addition, the model provides information about the extent to which a brand has achieved superiority or "ownership" of specific brand attributes. A larger BSA rating indicates stronger consumer identification with a positive characteristic, while a larger GBI component indicates that a brand's overall image is playing the primary role in the customer's rating.

The ways in which consumers retrieve① or compute personal brand ratings play an important role in the assessment. "When I say 'Starbucks,' that conjures② up certain associations that may not only be about the product," Dillon says. "It's also about the environment in which you consume the product, the merchandise, the setting, the

---

① retrieve [riˈtriːv] vt. 检索
② conjure [ˈkʌndʒə] vi. 激发

的实际联系，以及综合品牌印象（GBI）或者说消费者对品牌本身总体上是喜欢还是不喜欢。 这种分类能让公司理解总体印象对推动消费者的选择到底有多重要。

狄龙模型根据对客户的跟踪调查来调整品牌评级，这是它的一个优势。 例如，1 至 10 级处于从不支持到支持的数值范围。 此外，该模型提供了品牌在何种程度上已经取得某种具体品牌属性的优势或"所有权"。 专有品牌联想的评级越大，表明消费者越认同某个积极的特征，而综合品牌印象的评级越大，则表明品牌的整体形象在消费者的评级过程中发挥着主导作用。

消费者检索或估算个人品牌评级的方式在评估中发挥着重要的作用。 狄龙声称："当我说'星巴克'时会激发某些联想，也可能不只是对产品的联想。 它也是你对产品、商品、场景、社会氛围等环境的联想。 人的大脑建立了这些联想，人们据此做出选择，这也是衡量品牌实力的另一种方式。"

研究表明，综合品牌印象非常有利于在某一范畴内主导品牌。当人们根据若干属性评价市场领导者时，即使我们知道他们在所有属性方面并不都是最佳选择，但使其成为领导者的所有这些属性并不令人感到奇怪。 狄龙称之为"晕圈错误"，这种现象往往扭曲了公司在其品牌和产品属性方面建立的联系。

然而，由于创建品牌的大量工作出现在其营销活动中，所以认识到产品用途的社会背景甚至比拥有一种属性更加重要。 强大的品牌建立了情感依附效应。 他们试图发展为一种关系。 美国吉露果冻就是一个最好的例子。 果冻历来是可以让母亲和孩子联系在一起的产品。 他们记得的并不是对果冻的消费，而是准备过程、颜色、

social ambience. That these associations build in people's minds, and that people rely on them in making choices, is another measure of the strength of the brand."

Research demonstrates that general brand impressions heavily favor the dominant brand in a category. When people rate the market leader on a number of attributes, it's not surprising that it comes out the leader on all those attributes — even when we know they're not superior on all of them. Dillon calls this "halo error" and it often distorts the reflection of how well a company has developed an association between its brand and an attribute.

Yet because much of building a brand occurs in its marketing activities, recognizing the social context of a product's use can be even more important than owning an attribute. Strong brands build emotional attachments. They attempt to develop a relationship. Jell-O as a prime example. Jell-O historically is a product that allows mothers and children to bond. It's not the consumption of the Jell-O they remember, but the preparation, the colors, and the fun they had in making it — and Jell-O's marketing activities reflect this.

A product's physical attributes do not represent a sustainable marketplace advantage. Over time, competitors will imitate, patents will run out, buyers no longer can tell the difference among similar products. When the product effect dissipates, what's left is people's attachment to the brand. Strong brands recognize this.

(1,001 words)

他们在制作过程中所得到的乐趣。 果冻的营销活动反映了这一特点。

　　产品的物理属性并不代表可持续的市场优势。 随着时间的推移，竞争对手会仿效制造，专利权将消耗殆尽，买家不再能够说出类似产品之间的差别。 当产品效应消退，留下来的就是人们对品牌的联想。 强大的品牌会认识到这一点。

知识链接 🔍

The Coca-Cola Company 可口可乐公司。可口可乐公司成立于 1892 年，总部设在美国佐治亚州亚特兰大，是全球最大的饮料公司，拥有全球 48％市场占有率以及全球前三大饮料的两项。可口可乐在 200 个国家拥有 160 种饮料品牌，包括汽水、运动饮料、乳类饮品、果汁、茶和咖啡。

Starbucks 星巴克。星巴克咖啡公司成立于 1971 年，是世界领先的特种咖啡的零售商、烘焙者和星巴克品牌拥有者。旗下零售产品包括 30 多款全球顶级的咖啡豆、手工制作的浓缩咖啡和多款咖啡冷热饮料、新鲜美味的各式糕点食品以及丰富多样的咖啡机、咖啡杯等商品。

题　记

　　现代政治广告的实质就是由政府、政党、候选人及各种政治团体通过大众传播媒介付费购买时间、空间、机会和篇幅，直接向受众传输完全符合传者意愿的政治信息，欲要影响其政治态度或行为的传播过程。而商业广告是指商品经营者或服务提供者承担费用，通过一定的媒介和形式直接或间接地介绍推销商品或提供服务的广告。纯粹的曝光频率和持续不断的政治活动使政治广告的使用率成倍增长，而商业广告仍然财大气粗地统领广告领域的博大地盘。政治广告最显著的特征是内容消极和油腔滑调，而商业广告都会自愿遵守美国广告代理商协会颁布的"广告道德规范"。由于政治广告的实际效应推进了商业广告的相对吸引力，所以人们参与的政治活动加大了商业广告和政治广告之间的反差。

What Effect on Commercial Advertisers

Commercial advertising has always been a central feature of American culture. As encountered in the mass media, it is pervasive and inescapable. Most Americans take for granted the "rules" of commercial advertising, even though they may not be aware that any formal guidelines exist and may have little or no idea what the legal effect of such guidelines might be. Commercial advertisements are widely accepted as fair and legitimate marketing.

Contrast the world of political advertising. In recent years, political advertising has become essential to campaign strategy, at least in major campaigns, and many regard it as far more intrusive than routine commercial advertising. But the world of political advertising is very different from the world of commercial advertising. There really are no "rules" when it comes to the content and form of political advertising. Political advertisers are not accountable to any regulatory body, voluntary or otherwise, for the accuracy of their claims. They readily engage in so-called "comparative" advertising. They blatantly criticize their competitors. They complain incessantly about the fairness of the comments made about them, while their opponents are doing the same. There is no acknowledged forum for the review of these claims and counter-claims.

什么在影响商业广告商

商业广告一直是美国文化的一个核心特征。 大众传媒中的商业广告无处不在，不可避免。 大多数美国人对商业广告中的"规则"想当然，他们甚至不知道存不存在正式规则，也很少了解或者根本就不清楚这些规则会带来什么法律效果。 商业广告被广泛认为是公平合法的市场营销行为。

对比一下全球的政治广告。 近年来，政治广告已经成为必不可少的竞选策略，至少在重大竞选活动中是如此，而且很多人认为它比常规的商业广告更具干扰性。 但是，全球的政治广告与全球的商业广告有着天壤之别。 政治广告不存在内容和形式上的"规则"。政治广告商不用对任何监管机构负责，无论是出于自愿或是另有原因，也不需要对他们的声明的准确性负责。 政治广告具有所谓的"竞争性"。 他们明目张胆地批评他们的竞争对手。 他们和对手一样，总是抱怨别人对他们的评价不够公正。 没有一个公认的法庭来审议这些诉讼和反诉讼。 媒体试图通过"广告观察"对政治广告进行零星的检查，而这些报道本身就可能为公共政治助力。 大量的证

The press attempts to provide some sporadic① checks on political advertisers by running "ad-watch" reports, but these reports by their very nature tend to fuel public cynicism. Considerable evidence suggests that the negativity associated with contemporary political campaigns has created an "avoidance" mentality which is serving to shrink the electorate and the level of political participation generally.

The current state of political advertising has aroused considerable concern within the world of commercial advertising. Major advertising firms and professional associations have widely deplored② the lack of accountability of political advertisers and their unwillingness to adhere to a code of ethics. What exactly is Madison Avenue concerned about? Perhaps commercial advertisers fear that the apathy — and all too frequently, aversion — induced by political advertising campaigns may damage the credibility, and ultimately the persuasiveness, of more traditional forms of advertising. As Alex Kroll, former chairman of the American Association of Advertising Agencies, put it: "We must stop politicians from ruining our reputation." Kroll's was not a solitary voice. The former American Association of Advertising Agencies (4A) chair John O'Toole claimed that political ads were "giving advertising a bad name." Burt Manning went so far as to assert that the "smear③ and scare" tactics of political advertisers meant that "today, the issue is survival of brand advertising". Our goal is to provide some evidence on the issue of whether political advertising, does, in fact, "contaminate" commercial advertising.

---

① sporadic [spə'rædik] *adj.* 零星的
② deplored [di'plɔː] *vt.* 悲悼
③ smear [smiə] *n.* 污迹

据表明，当代政治运动的负面影响造成了"回避"的心态，总体上缩减了参与政治的选民，同时也降低了水平。

政治广告的当前状况已经引起了人们对商业广告的广泛关注。大型广告公司和专业协会普遍谴责政治广告商推卸责任，不愿意遵守职业道德守则。究竟什么是麦迪逊大道关注的焦点？商业广告商或许忧心忡忡，担心政治广告竞争导致的商业广告冷漠感会损害其信誉，最终削弱更多传统广告的说服力。正如美国广告代理协会的前任董事长亚历克斯·克罗尔所说的那样，"我们必须阻止政客损毁我们的声誉"。无独有偶，前美国广告代理商协会的董事长约翰·奥托尔宣称，政治广告"正在败坏商业广告的名声"。伯尔特·马宁甚至断言："泼脏水和恐吓"的政治广告战术意味着"事关当今广告品牌的存亡"。我们的目标是提供一些证据，证明政治广告究竟是否在事实上"污染"了商业广告。

纯粹的曝光频率和持续不断的政治活动使政治广告的使用率成倍增长，但与商业广告相比，政治广告仍然显得微不足道。大选的总费用约达 25 亿美元。这个数字低于美国大公司的年度广告预算。竞选的高峰时期，前 75 家媒体市场的电视广告只有不到百分之一是由政治候选人或组织赞助的。显然，公众对这些广告的反感是基于其他因素而不单单是因为其太频繁。

当代政治竞选广告最显著的特征是内容消极和油腔滑调。政治广告商经常采取所谓的"对比"方式，在广告中批评甚至嘲笑对方

Even though the use of political advertising has spread exponentially①, both in terms of the sheer frequency of exposure and the increased length of political campaigns, political advertising is still miniscule② compared with commercial advertising. The total cost of the election amounted to approximately $ 2.5 billion. This figure is less than the annual advertising budget for major U. S. corporations. During the height of the campaign, fewer than one percent of all televised advertisements in the top 75 media markets were sponsored by political candidates or organizations. Clearly, the public's distaste for these advertisements is based on factors other than sheer frequency.

The most distinctive feature of contemporary political campaign advertisements is the negativity of their content and tone. Political advertisers frequently engage in so-called "comparative" advertising in which the opposing candidate's program and performance are criticized and even ridiculed. Highlighting the opponent's liabilities and weaknesses usually takes precedence over identifying the sponsor's program and strengths. In the most comprehensive tracking of campaign advertising to date, scholars at the Annenberg School of Communication have found that such "negative" advertising makes up approximately one-third of all campaign ads used in presidential campaigns. The level of negativity is actually significantly greater when one considers frequency-weighted indicators of content. For instance, while fewer than one-half of the ads produced by the major candidates featured negative appeals this year, these appeals accounted for some seventy percent of the candidates' ad buys. While we do not have comparable data for any commercial

---

① exponentially [ekspə'nenʃəli] *adv.* 成指数地
② miniscule ['miniskju:l] *adj.* 小字的

候选人的节目和表现。 他们强调对手的不足和弱点，而不是肯定赞助商的节目和优势。 安能宝传播学院的学者对迄今为止的竞选广告进行了最全面的跟踪，他们发现这种"消极"的广告约占所有总统竞选广告的三分之一。 值得关注的是，如果考虑内容的频率加权指标，消极的程度实际上更高。 例如，虽然今年关于主要候选人负面呼声的广告占了不到一半，但是这些诉求却占了候选人购买广告的约 70% 的份额。 虽然我们没有任何关于商业广告竞争的参照数据，"比较"元素也许不太可能这么显著，但跟商业广告比起来，政治广告在内容上更加消极。

政治广告不同于商业广告，他们不会为了设法保护公众免受不准确和毫无根据的主张而遵守任何规范或程序。 而所有的商业广告人都会自愿遵守美国广告代理商协会颁布的"广告道德规范"。 该规范包括处理不实和误导性言论投诉的条款。 全国广告评估委员针对特定的广告投诉进行审查和仲裁。 对双方的证据审查之后，仲裁小组可能发现有效投诉，并要求相关人对有问题的广告予以修改和废止。 仲裁小组还可以将投诉提交给有关的政府机构。 如果广告商不遵从修改和终止要求，该小组可以发布"谨防违规者"标识，确认违规的广告商。

政治广告商不希望受制于自愿准则的约束。 实际上，第一修正案的保护措施不可能强行限制政治广告的内容。 美国政治顾问协会无意于鼓励任何形式的自制。 这样的结果造成了全民自由的环境，

advertising campaign, the "comparative" element is unlikely to be so prominent; when compared with commercial ads, political ads are much more negative in content.

Unlike commercial advertisers, political advertises do not adhere to any codes or procedures intended to protect the public from inaccurate and unsubstantiated claims. All commercial advertisers voluntarily subscribe to a "code of advertising ethics" administered by the 4A. This code includes provisions for dealing with complaints of false or misleading claims. Complaints directed at specific ads are reviewed and arbitrated by a panel appointed by the National Advertising Review Board. After reviewing the evidence from both sides, the panel may find the complaint to be valid and require that the ad in question be modified or discontinued. The panel may also refer the complaint to the appropriate governmental agency. If the advertiser fails to comply with a request for modification or termination, the panel may issue a "notice of noncompliance" identifying the advertiser.

Political advertisers are not subject to comparable voluntary guidelines. First Amendment protections make it virtually impossible to impose involuntary restraints on the content of political advertising. The American Association of Political Consultants has shown no inclination to encourage any form of self-restraint. The result is a free-for-all environment in which candidates repeatedly attack and counter-attack the claims of their competitors. The only accountability is provided by the press, in the form of sporadic "ad-watch" news reports that scrutinize specific ads for their accuracy. The very nature of ad-watch journalism, however, is bound to exacerbate① public cynicism over the fairness and

---

① exacerbate [eksˈæsə(ː)beit] vt. 使……恶化

在这样的环境下，候选人可以一而再、再而三地攻击和反击竞争对手的主张。 其唯一的责任是按照"广告监视"的指示，实时监控特定新闻报道的准确性。 然而，广告监控方式监管新闻的核心本质必然加剧公众对政治广告的公正度和可信度的冷嘲热讽。

政治广告的辐射效果会不会蔓延到整个商业广告领域？ 我们试图通过控制政治广告的曝光率、然后测量参与者对政治和商业广告竞争的态度来解答这个问题。 为了评估消极的政治竞争对观众的政治以及产品信心的影响，我们还控制了政治广告的定调。 我们的研究结果表明，一般而言，接触政治广告，尤其是消极的政治广告，增强了看客对商业广告的相对信赖。 人们不会把对政治广告的厌恶带入商业广告领域。 他们在接触政治广告后也没有表现出对商业广告的更加青睐。 但是，由于竞选加剧了观众对政治广告的厌烦，它的实际效应就是推进了商业广告的相对吸引力。 所以，参与政治活动加大了商业广告和政治广告之间的反差。

知识链接 🔍

Madison Avenue 麦迪逊大道。纽约曼哈顿区的一条著名大街。美国许多广告公司的总部都集中在这条街上，因此这条街逐渐成为了美国广告业的代名词。

4A 美国广告代理商协会(American Association of Advertising Agencies)。

credibility of political advertising.

Does the fallout from exposure to political advertising spread to commercial advertising in general? We attempt to answer this question experimentally, by manipulating exposure to political advertising and then measuring participants' attitudes towards political and commercial ad campaigns. We also manipulate the tone of political advertising in order to assess the impact of negative political campaigns on the audience's confidence in political and product advertisers. Our results indicate that exposure to political advertising in general — and negative political advertising in particular — strengthens viewers' relative confidence in commercial advertising. People do not assimilate their generally unfavorable ratings of political ads to the commercial advertising arena. Nor do they express more favorable attitudes toward commercial advertising in the aftermath of exposure to political advertising. However, because campaigns heighten distaste for political advertising, the net effect is to boost the relative appeal of commercial advertising. Thus, exposure to political campaigns enlarges the contrast between commercial and political advertising.

(1,091 words)

美国广告代理商协会成立于 1917 年的美国圣路易斯，是全世界最早的广告代理商协会。该协会定有协会自律规则《实践标准和创作守则》，违反会规者就要被开除会籍，以此约束会员公司遵守广告道德准则。在全球营业额前 25 位的广告公司中，公司总部设在美国的占 15 家。它们都是该协会的会员。协会成员承担着全美 70%~80%的广告业务量。

题 记

　　由于小企业的资本投资和人员雇用在某种程度上依赖于他们的贷款准入，小企业贷款的房地产诱导阻力使就业和投资计划陷入低迷的困境。小企业主将自己拥有的不动产，即房地产抵押给银行，以拿到更多的贷款支持自身的商业活动，很多小企业主甚至将家庭的房产用来抵押。随着房地产价格的下跌以及通货膨胀的提高，银行的财务也陷入危机，结果对整个社会的经济产生了不良影响。由此可见，在促进经济发展的一系列政策中，有些方针犹如一把双刃剑，既有好的一面，但是也隐藏着不利的一面，这就要求人们要更加慎重地尊重经济发展的客观规律，切忌急功近利。

Real Estate's Link to the Small Business Credit Crunch

It's no secret that small businesses in the U. S. face difficulties accessing credit. According to a survey of a random sample of 751 small businesses conducted by Gallup for the National Federation of Independent Business Research Foundation this year, 44% of small businesses seeking credit received only some or none of the money they sought. This level of credit access compares poorly with the last year, when nine of every 10 companies seeking credit received it.

While there is broad agreement that a small business credit problem exists, there is less consensus① about its causes. As a result, formulating viable solutions has proved difficult. Although many factors are contributing to current credit problems, one that is under-appreciated is the degree to which small business credit is linked to difficulties in the commercial and residential② real estate markets.

Real estate plays an important role in small business lending. Falling real estate prices impinge on the ability of small employers to borrow the

---

① consensus [kən'sensəs] *n.* 舆论
② residential [ˌrezi'denʃəl] *adj.* 住宅的

小型企业商业信贷与房地产的联系

　　美国的小型企业难以获得信贷早已不是什么秘密。 盖洛普今年随机抽取了 751 家小型企业的样本，为全国商业联合独立研究基金会做了一项调查。 研究显示，44% 的谋求信贷的小型企业要么只收到了部分贷款，要么没有丝毫的斩获。 这种信贷准入水平与去年相比要差得多，当时每 10 家谋求信贷的公司有 9 家收到贷款。

　　虽然人们对小企业信贷存在的问题达成了广泛的共识，但对造成这种现象的原因却少有人认同。 其结果是难以制定切实可行的解决方案。 尽管导致目前信贷问题的因素很多，但小企业信贷与商业和住宅房地产市场困境的相关度未能获得足够的重视仍然是其中的因素之一。

　　房地产在小企业贷款中扮演着重要角色。 下跌的房地产价格促使那些能力较小的业主需要借钱运营公司，因为小企业利用房地产获取各种各样的贷款。 根据美国独立企业联合会的研究，21% 的小业主为了商业目的抵押房地产，11% 的小业主利用房地产做抵押，获取其他的商业资产。

　　此外，根据美国独立企业联合会的调查，在放松信贷的期间，

money they need to fund their operations because small businesses use real estate to obtain credit in a variety of ways. According to the NFIB study, 21% of small employers have mortgaged real estate for business purposes and 11% use real estate as collateral for other business assets.

Moreover, according to the NFIB, during the period of easy credit, some small business owners obtained loans by using real estate whose value turned out to be inflated. As a result, the owners were able to borrow more than their credit, and perhaps their businesses, could support. When real estate prices fell, the value of the collateral pledged against these loans dropped, and some these loans could no longer be supported. In fact, 13% of small business owners have a property that is under water, according to the NFIB survey.

Falling real estate prices also have weakened small business balance sheets and made them less creditworthy borrowers. Lenders have responded to the worsened financials by cutting back on credit to small businesses. Thus, even when small businesses seek loans to pursue promising business opportunities, their weakened balance sheets mean fewer of them can borrow than when credit was easier.

Personal borrowing is a big part of small business finance. To obtain capital to finance their business operations, many small business owners make use of their personal credit. Analysis of the Federal Reserve Survey of Consumer Finances shows that 18% of business-owning households used personal assets to guarantee or collateralize① business debt.

Homes are the main assets that small business owners can pledge to

---

① collateralize [kə'lætərəlaiz] vt. 以······作抵押

一些小业主利用抵押不动产获取贷款，这些不动产的价值造成了通货膨胀。 结果，业主借的钱比贷款还多，超出了企业的承受能力。当房地产价格下跌时，之前抵押物的价值坚决抵制这些贷款下降，有些贷款将不再被支持。 事实上，根据美国独立企业联合会的调查，13% 的小业主随时可能失去产权。

房地产价格的下跌也削弱了小企业的资产负债表，使他们成为信誉不佳的借贷人。 放款方与恶化的金融环境相呼应，削减了小企业的贷款。 因此，即使小企业寻求贷款，以捕捉有希望的商业机会，但摇摇欲坠的资产负债表却意味着他们中只有较少的人比较容易获得贷款。

个人借贷是小企业融资的一个重要部分。 为了筹措资金资助企业的运营，许多小企业主利用个人信誉贷款。 美联储"消费者财务状况调查"分析称，18% 的私营业主家庭使用过个人资产为商业债务担保或抵押。

家庭资产是最主要的财产，小业主可以用来抵押获得贷款，这种做法使住宅地产成为小企业融资的重要来源。 美国独立企业联合会在"小型企业信用在严重衰退"的报告中指出，16% 的小企业主用住宅抵押贷款为企业提供融资，6% 的小企业主用家庭资产抵押贷款筹措营业资产。

在房屋净值贷款泛滥的时候，小企业主的贷款用得不成比例。美联储"消费者财务状况调查"分析称，个体经营户的房屋净值贷款份额增加了 182% ，相比之下，受雇于他人的经营者只有 121% 。此外，房屋净值贷款债务的中值在个人经营中增加了 48% ，但是同一时期受雇于他人的经营者缩减了 29% 。

obtain loans, making residential real estate an important source of small business finance. According to the NFIB's report, Small Business Credit in a Deep Recession①, 16% of small employers use a residential mortgage to finance a business and 6% use their homes to collateralize business assets.

During the home equity lending boom, small business owners were disproportionate users of these loans. According to an analysis of the Federal Reserve Survey of Consumer Finances, the share of self-employed with home equity debt increased 182%, compared with only 121% among those employed by others. Moreover, the median value of home equity debt increased 48% among the self-employed but shrank 29% among those employed by others over the same period.

Because home values account for a large portion of the value of household assets, declining home prices reduce the amount of personal credit that small employers can obtain. As Federal Reserve Board Governor Elizabeth Duke explained in recent Congressional testimony, with declines in house prices and consequent weakened household balance sheets, the ability of many small business owners to borrow has likely been impaired.

In some cases, homes are no longer an asset against which small business owners can borrow at all. The NFIB reports that 9% of small business owners are underwater on their home mortgages. Many banks are suffering from heavy exposure to nonperforming② real estate loans that have weakened their financial positions. Unfortunately, small business borrowing is relatively concentrated in the banks with the highest exposure

---

① recession [ri'seʃən] n. 衰退
② nonperforming [ˌnɔnpə'fɔːmiŋ] adj.【银行业】无息的,不支付利息的

因为房屋价值占家庭资产价值的很大一部分，所以家庭资产价格下滑将大量减少小业主可能获得的个人信贷。 美国联邦储备委员会理事伊丽莎白·杜克最近在国会听证会上解释说，不断下降的住宅价格和随之而来的虚弱的家庭资产负债很可能已经破坏了许多小企业主的借款能力。

在某些情况下，房屋不再完全是资助小业主借贷的资产。 根据美国独立企业联合会的报告，9% 的小业主的住房抵押岌岌可危。许多银行饱受不良房地产贷款的拖累，这种状况严重削弱了他们的财务。 不幸的是，小型商业借贷相对集中的银行受到了不良房地产贷款最严重的影响。 根据国会监督小组"商业地产损失和对金融稳定的风险"报告，就所有的小企业商业贷款而言，与小企业往来关系最频繁的较小的银行，提供了约 40% 的贷款，即商业房地产贷款超过一级资本的三倍。 大量小型商业银行的不良房地产贷款使亚特兰大联邦储备银行的经济学家们对"小企业借贷的近期增长前景"深感悲观失望。

此外，小企业贷款目前已经出现了恶性循环。 国会督查小组报告对此做出了解释，不断下滑的房地产价值阻碍了小企业借贷。 没有借贷能力引起更多的小企业破产。 较高的破产率继而导致降低房地产价值的空置率。 假使小企业主依赖商业和住宅房地产价值资助企业，并将其主要贷款人置于不良房地产贷款的高度风险下，如果不处理困扰这个国家的房地产问题，很难相信小企业信贷问题可以得到妥善解决。

近期对小业主的调查显示，由于小企业的资本投资和人员雇用在某种程度上依赖于他们的贷款准入，小企业贷款的房地产诱导阻

to bad real estate loans. According to the Congressional Oversight Panel report *Commercial Real Estate Losses and the Risk to Financial Stability*, smaller banks with the highest exposure — commercial real estate loans in excess of three times Tier 1 capital — provide around 40% of all small business loans. The heavy exposure of small business lenders to bad real estate loans makes Federal Reserve Bank of Atlanta research economists pessimistic about the "near-term outlook for growth in small business borrowing".

Moreover, a vicious cycle has now emerged in small business credit. As the Congressional Oversight Panel report explains, declining real estate values hinder small business borrowing. The inability to borrow causes more small businesses to fail. The higher failure rate, in turn, results in vacancies that reduce real estate values. Given the reliance of small business owners on commercial and residential real estate values to finance their businesses and the high exposure of their primary lenders to bad real estate loans, it's difficult to see how small business credit problems can be resolved without a fix to the real estate problems plaguing this country.

Because small business capital investment and hiring depend, in part, on their access to credit, the real estate-induced drag on small business credit has led to the depressed hiring and investment plans reported by small business owners in recent surveys. Given the role that small business has played in stimulating economic recoveries historically, that's bad news for all of us.

(935 words)

力使就业和投资计划陷入低迷的困境。 考虑到小企业在刺激经济恢复中历来扮演的角色，对我们所有人而言，这真是个不幸的消息。

知识链接

Federal Reserve Bank 美国联邦储备银行。美国联邦储备银行是世界上最具实力的银行，总部位于自由大道 33 号，还包括 12 家银行及其分布在全美各地的 25 家地区分行。尽管它最初设立的目的是为了稳定和保护美国的银行系统，但其目前的主要职责却是控制通货膨胀。美联储由一个 7 人组成的总裁委员会负责管理，所有委员均由总裁予以委任。每个委员的任期长达 14 年。总裁委员会下设 1 名主席和 1 名副主席，其任期均为 4 年。由 12 名委员组成的联邦公开市场委员会则是一个具有重要影响力的组织，该委员会每年召开八次会议，研讨美国的经济和货币政策。

题　记

　　产品和企业的品牌符号在全球文化中承载着品质卓越和责任担当的光环。万宝路"西部牛仔"代表的是自由精神，大红鹰"V"代表永远胜利，NIKE 的"对勾"代表叛逆的心理，可口可乐的红色代表活力。令人扼腕叹息的是，全球品牌化的光彩在人们对跨国公司的围追堵截中黯然失色，品牌符号被视为既能造福、又可作恶的强大机构。可口可乐、麦当劳和耐克之类的品牌已经成为反全球化浪潮的出气筒：愤怒的示威者砸碎了瑞士达沃斯麦当劳出口的玻璃门，踩踏着西雅图的可乐罐。消费者对全球品牌的认知迫使企业在文化背景下思考全球文化的符号，了解好莱坞和宝莱坞电影、美国有线新闻网和卡达尔半岛电视台新闻报道、嘻哈音乐和苏非派音乐等世界不同文化之间的区别。

Brand Symbols
in the Global Culture

When a brand is marketed around the world, that fact alone gives it an aura of excellence — and a set of obligations. To maximize the value of global reach, companies must manage both.

It's time to rethink global branding. More than two decades ago, Harvard Business School professor Theodore Levitt provocatively declared in a HBR article, "The Globalization of Markets," that a global market for uniform products and services had emerged. He argued that corporations should exploit the "economics of simplicity" and grow by selling standardized products all over the world. Although Levitt did not explicitly discuss branding, managers interpreted his ideas to mean that transnational companies should standardize products, packaging, and communication to achieve a least-common-denominator[①] positioning that would be effective across cultures. From that commonsense standpoint, global branding was only about saving costs and ensuring consistent

---

① least common denominator 最小公分母

全球文化中的品牌符号

一个品牌推广到全球，就意味着它戴上了品质卓越的光环，并需要承担一系列的责任。为了品牌价值在全球范围内最大化，公司必须两者兼顾。

现在是重新思考全球品牌化的时候了。二十多年前，哈佛商学院教授西奥多·利维特在《哈佛商业评论》发表题为"市场全球化"的文章，宣称统一产品和服务的全球市场已经出现，这种观点颇具煽动性。他认为，公司应该开发"简单经济学"，通过在全世界出售标准化产品获得发展。虽然利维特没有明确讨论品牌化，企业管理者却把他的观点解读为：跨国公司应该实现产品、包装和营销宣传的标准化，构成有效跨越不同文化的"最小公分母式"的品牌定位。从常识上讲，全球品牌化只是节约成本和确保与客户持续沟通。这个观点在 20 世纪 80 年代颇受欢迎，当一些国家对外国竞争对手开放市场时，美国和日本公司就曾试图运用全球品牌和行销方案渗入其中。

虽然世界经济持续一体化，但全球品牌化的实验却很快放缓。公司的"最小公分母"理念带来的产品和营销宣传，难以打动大多

customer communication. The idea proved popular in the 1980s, when several countries opened up to foreign competition and American and Japanese corporations tried to penetrate those markets with global brands and marketing programs.

While the world economy continued to integrate, experiments with global branding soon slowed. Consumers in most countries had trouble relating to the generic products and communications that resulted from companies' least-common-denominator thinking. Executives therefore rushed to fashion hybrid strategies. They strove for global scale on backstage activities such as technology, production, and organization but made sure product features, communications, distribution, and selling techniques were customized to local consumer tastes. Such "glocal" strategies have ruled marketing ever since.

Global branding has lost more luster recently because transnational companies have been under virtual siege①. The evidence is on the streets and in stores all around us. Brands like Coca-Cola, McDonald's, and Nike have become lightning rods for antiglobalization protests. Who can forget the images of angry demonstrators smashing the windows of a McDonald's outlet in Davos, Switzerland, or stomping Coke cans in Seattle? Political parties and nongovernmental organizations (NGOs) have drawn bull's-eyes on transnational companies because they're the most visible and vulnerable symbols of globalization's side effects, such as

---

① siege [siːdʒ] *n.* 包围

数国家的消费者。 企业主管们于是匆忙转向流行混合战略。 他们力求让技术、生产和组织等后台活动达到全球规模，但同时又根据当地消费者的品位，量身定制产品特色、营销宣传和销售方法。 这些"全球本土化"战略至今仍在营销领域占统治地位。

由于跨国公司一直受到围追堵截，全球品牌化的光彩最近已经黯然失色。 在我们周围的街道上和商店里都可以找到证据。 可口可乐、麦当劳和耐克之类的品牌已经成为反全球化浪潮的出气筒。谁能忘记愤怒的示威者砸碎瑞士达沃斯麦当劳出口的玻璃门抑或西雅图踩踏可乐罐的事件？ 政党和非政府组织（NGOs）将跨国公司视作"靶心"，因为他们是全球化副作用下最显而易见和易受伤害的符号，例如剥削性工资、环境污染和文化帝国主义。 美国这个超级大国发起阿富汗和伊拉克战争后，美国外交政策的反对声迭起，这进一步动摇了跨国公司的根基，因为国际品牌顾问"国际品牌集团"发布的"全球最具价值品牌前百强"中，美国占据 62 个品牌。 大多数跨国公司的本能反应自然是规避风险。

但是，全球品牌总是引人注目，更为重要的是，它们在消费者的心目中具有影响力。 事实上，大多数跨国公司没有意识到，人们对它们刮目相看，认为它们与众不同。 由于全球品牌无处不在，它们被视为既能造福、又可作恶的强大机构。 我们对 41 个国家的 3 300 名客户进行了一项调查，发现大多数人出于对品牌全球品质差异的考虑，选择全球品牌而不是其他品牌。 公司不可忽视自身品牌的全球特性，必须学会经营这些特性。 这一点很关键，因为大多数

exploitative wages, pollution, and cultural imperialism. The opposition to U. S. foreign policy that arose after the superpower went to war in Afghanistan and Iraq has further shaken companies, because, according to global brand consultancy Interbrand, 62 of the world's 100 most valuable global brands were American. Naturally, the instinctive reaction of most transnational companies has been to try to fly below the radar①.

But global brands can't escape notice — they've never been more salient② in the minds of consumers. In fact, most transnational corporations don't realize that people view them differently than they do other firms. Because of their pervasiveness, global brands are seen as powerful institutions — capable of doing great good and causing considerable harm. When we conducted a research project involving 3,300 consumers in 41 countries, we found that most people choose one global brand over another because of differences in the brands' global qualities. Rather than ignore the global characteristics of their brands, firms must learn to manage those characteristics. That's critical, because future growth for most companies will likely come from foreign markets. Developed countries in North America, Europe, and East Asia accounted for 15% of the world's population of 6.3 billion. By 2030, according to the World Bank, the planet's population will rise to 9 billion, with 90% of people living in developing countries.

---

① fly below the radar 逃过一劫
② salient ['seiljənt] *adj.* 显著的

公司未来的增长可能来自海外市场。 北美、欧洲和东亚发达国家占全球 63 亿人口的 15% 。 据世界银行的估计，到 2030 年，世界人口将上升到 90 亿，90% 的人生活在发展中国家。

为了把握消费者对全球品牌的认知，公司应该在文化背景下思考全球文化的符号。 利维特描述的推动力没有产生一个单一的世界市场，而是制造了全球文化。 文化主要是通过交流产生，依靠交流传承。 现代社会有多种交流形式：报纸杂志文章、广播电视节目、国际互联网、书籍、电影、音乐、艺术，当然还有广告和营销。 几十年来，各国的文化主要在境内流通，以帮助建立强大的民族文化。 20 世纪末，大量的流行文化走向世界。 由于国家融入了世界经济体系，跨境旅游和劳动力流动随之增加，电视节目、电影和音乐对消费者逐渐普及，互联网呈爆炸式增长。 这些因素迫使人们正视他们与其他文化以及自身文化的联系。 例如，全球各地的消费者必须了解好莱坞和宝莱坞电影、美国有线新闻网和卡达尔半岛电视台新闻报道、嘻哈音乐和苏非派音乐等世界不同文化之间的区别。

全球文化的兴起并不意味着消费者分享同样的品位和价值观。 恰恰相反，尽管不同国家的人通常拥有相互冲突的观点，但他们在相互交谈时会借助于共享符号。 交谈的重要符号之一是全球品牌。 娱乐明星、运动名人和政治家等全球品牌已经成为全世界消费者的通用语。 人们对跨国公司或喜爱或厌恶，但却不能忽视他们的存在。 许多消费者对跨国公司的政治权利心存敬畏，因为这些公司的销售额比一些小国家的国内生产总值还要多，它们极大地影响着人

To grasp how consumers perceive global brands, companies should think about symbols in the global culture in cultural terms. The forces that Levitt described didn't produce a homogeneous world market; they produced a global culture. Culture is created and preserved mainly by communication. In modern societies, communication takes many forms: newspaper and magazine articles, television and radio broadcasts, Internet content, books, films, music, art, and, of course, advertising and marketing communications. For decades, communication had circulated mostly within the borders of countries, helping to build strong national cultures. Toward the end of the twentieth century, much of popular culture became global. As nations integrated into the world economy, cross-border tourism and labor mobility rose; TV channels, movies, and music became universally available to consumers; and, more recently, Internet growth has exploded. Those factors force people to see themselves in relation to other cultures as well as their own. For instance, consumers everywhere have to make sense of the world vis-à-vis Hollywood and Bollywood films, CNN and al-Jazeera news reports, hip-hop and Sufi music.

The rise of a global culture doesn't mean that consumers share the same tastes or values. Rather, people in different nations, often with conflicting viewpoints, participate in a shared conversation, drawing upon shared symbols. One of the key symbols in that conversation is the global brand. Like entertainment stars, sports celebrities, and politicians, global brands have become a lingua franca for consumers all

们的生活以及社区福利、国家和这个星球。 不足为奇的是，消费者将某些特征归因于全球品牌，并使用这些属性作为标准而做出购买决定。

消费者小心翼翼地关注着跨国公司之间进行的激烈的品质战，他们对战胜方印象深刻。 俄罗斯的一位焦点小组参与者告诉我们："越多的人买这个牌子，这个牌子的质量就越好。"葡萄牙的一位消费者同意这个观点："我喜爱全球品牌，因为他们的质量通常比其他产品更好，厂商更有保证。"这种观点经常成为全球品牌收取额外费用的理由。 一位泰国的参与者指出：全球品牌"昂贵但物有所值"。 消费者还认为，跨国公司试图通过开发新产品与对手竞争，利用技术突破超越对手。 一位印度人认为，全球品牌"活力无限，并正在不断提高自己的品位"。 一个澳大利亚人补充道，全球品牌"令人更加兴奋，因为他们持续不断地推出新产品，而你也知道地方品牌是怎么回事"。

知识链接 🔍

Hollywood 好莱坞。好莱坞位于美国加利福尼亚州洛杉矶市市区西北郊，是洛杉矶的邻近地区，约有 30 万居民。但由于当地发达的娱乐工业，现在"好莱坞"一词往往直接用来指美国加州南部的电影工业。好莱坞生产的影片不仅满足美利坚合众国电影市场的需要，还出口到世界各地，不仅输出了美利坚合众国的文化，更为好莱坞投资人带来了丰厚的利润。

Bollywood 宝莱坞。宝莱坞是位于印度孟买的广受欢迎的电影工业基地的

over the world. People may love or hate transnational companies, but they can't ignore them. Many consumers are awed by the political power of companies that have sales greater than the GDPs of small nations and that have a powerful impact on people's lives as well as the welfare of communities, nations, and the planet itself. Not surprisingly, consumers ascribe certain characteristics to global brands and use those attributes as criteria while making purchase decisions.

Consumers watch carefully the fierce battles that transnational companies wage over quality and are impressed by the victors. A focus-group participant in Russia told us: "The more people who buy a brand, the better quality it is." A Spanish consumer agreed: "I like global brands because they usually offer more quality and better guarantees than other products." That perception often serves as a rationale for global brands to charge premiums. Global brands "are expensive, but the price is reasonable when you think of the quality," pointed out a Thai participant. Consumers also believe that transnational companies compete by trying to develop new products and breakthrough technologies faster than rivals. Global brands "are very dynamic, always upgrading themselves," said an Indian. An Australian added that global brands "are more exciting because they come up with new products all the time, whereas you know what you'll get with local ones."

(1,016 words)

别名，它也被称作"印地语（Hindi）的影院"。宝莱坞和印度其他几个主要影视基地构成了印度的庞大电影业，每年出产的电影数量和售出的电影票数量居全世界第一，对印度以至整个印度次大陆、中东以及非洲和东南亚的一部分的流行文化都有重要的影响，并通过南亚的移民输出传播到整个世界。